Real World Mindfulness for Beginners

Real World Mindfulness

for Beginners

Navigate
Daily Life
One Practice
at a Time

Edited by Brenda Salgado

FALL RIVER PRESS

New York

FALL RIVER PRESS

New York

An Imprint of Sterling Publishing Co., Inc.
1166 Avenue of the Americas
New York, NY 10036

ISBN 978-1-4351-6708-7

For information about custom editions, special sales, and premium
and corporate purchases, please contact Sterling Special Sales at
800-805-5489 or specialsales@sterlingpublishing.com.

Manufactured in the United States of America

2 4 6 8 10 9 7 5 3 1

sterlingpublishing.com

This book is dedicated to my grandmother
Maria Paula Guevara Galan. Thank you
for guiding me on this path of spiritual
teaching and healing service in the world.

Contents

Editor's Introduction

Warm greetings and welcome. Perhaps you purchased this book because you are looking to navigate your life with more joy, because you or your loved ones are facing difficult challenges, or because you want to feel more centered as conditions are changing in the world. Perhaps you are a leader seeking to be more mindful and productive in the way you show up at work, or someone purchased this book as a gift for you. Whatever way you came to find yourself reading these pages, I am honored to introduce you to a wise and diverse group of teachers who have demonstrated a commitment to sharing mindfulness practices with people from all walks of life.

As we hold fear and sorrow about violence, injustice, war, economic uncertainty, and planetary crisis, can meditation help us be more present with the challenges we face individually and collectively?

Mindfulness is a state of being in which we focus our attention on the present moment, encouraging a nonjudgmental and heightened awareness of our feelings, thoughts, and sensations. Mindfulness seems to be the latest trend, promising us less stress, greater productivity, and a happier life, and increasingly, scientific and medical researchers confirm the many benefits of mindfulness practices like meditation. While the roots of mindfulness can be found in many spiritual traditions, at its core, it holds promise for all humanity, especially in the times we find ourselves in.

In 2010, I was invited to the State of Contemplative Practice in America meeting at the Fetzer Institute in Kalamazoo, Michigan. This gathering had a huge impact on my life. Twenty-seven leaders from across the country were invited to discuss how mindfulness was changing our culture and the way we live, work, and play together. Some attendees supported contemplative practices in their Christian, Jewish, Buddhist, or Sufi tradition, while others were leading secular-based mindfulness programs in education, end-of-life care, the legal system, leadership development, and social justice movements.

Throughout the meeting, different people led the group in meditation. Sitting in a large circle with a Buddhist teacher, a Franciscan monk, a Jewish rabbi, a Sufi scholar, and others, I settled into a deep understanding that mindfulness belongs to many traditions and cultures, and that these practices can serve to remind us of our connection to the earth and to our shared humanity.

Since that time, I have deepened my own practice and teaching as a spiritual leader, healer, and meditator. I currently serve on the boards of two organizations that bring mindfulness practices and writings to different communities. In the recent past, I served as the director of the East Bay Meditation Center, a national model committed to gift economy, diversity, and inclusive community building. In all of these places, I am constantly learning from others about the world we are hungry for and want to build together—one where all of us belong and thrive, and where all beings are free.

Perhaps you or someone you love is facing a serious illness, a job loss, or struggling with addiction. Perhaps you hold fear and sorrow around violence, injustice, and economic and climate uncertainty in our society. Our hope is that mindfulness practices can help you be more present with the challenges you face right now and to listen more deeply, cultivate creativity and curiosity, weather changes with more dignity and grace, and create a better world for future generations.

We can start right here, right now, to bring mindfulness into our lives in small but life-changing ways. Whether it is Maia Duerr's caring with intention practice, Yingzhao Liu's breathing meditation, or affirmations on belonging taught to me by an indigenous elder, I hope you will find accessible discussions and practical exercises to reduce stress and cultivate beauty and peace in your life. The exercises in these chapters are easy to implement and take just a few minutes during your busy day.

one

The Mindful Moment

Brenda Salgado

is founder of the Nepantla Center for Healing and Renewal and serves on the Lion's Roar Foundation board. She was previously director of the East Bay Meditation Center in Oakland, California.

Several years ago, I suddenly fell ill. For almost three weeks, I was anemic and incredibly weak, and needed help with the simplest of tasks. I remember feeling frustrated at how little I was accomplishing and how many things I was falling behind on. I imagine you have experienced similar frustrations juggling work, family, and life in general. We can't always control the conditions surrounding us, but we can cultivate practices to cope and respond with a sense of choice, integrity, and wisdom.

One Mindful Moment to a Lifetime of Freedom

One of the reasons mindfulness can be so helpful is that we are often unaware of how our thoughts, feelings, and unconscious assumptions can limit our perceptions of what is happening. We often have habitual thoughts and running stories in our minds that we think are objectively "the truth." These thoughts can keep us from seeing the bigger picture. This is why pausing to take a breath can help during difficult exchanges. In this book, we think about mindfulness as the ability to be present in the current moment, with awareness of our thoughts, emotions, and sensations in the body and what is happening in our environment. Another aspect of mindfulness is cultivating curiosity and openness with what is present in you and around you.

During my health challenge, mindfulness helped me notice my frustration and shame, so I decided to extend myself the compassion I often show others. I tuned into my body's request for iron-rich foods and plant medicines, worked with my doctor and acupuncturist to restore my body to health, and, as much as I wanted to be in control, I communicated with family and coworkers about the rest and support I needed. I was able to recuperate quickly, slowing down and accepting support from others, despite my habitual thoughts. My husband shared afterward that it felt good to take care of me, and I was touched by his honesty.

Many cultures have practices that cultivate stillness and mindfulness. Whether it is contemplative prayer in Christian traditions, the Amidah in Judaism, or the sweat lodge ceremonies of some Native American cultures, people around the world have long sought to develop mental, emotional, physical, and spiritual awareness. Buddhism is perhaps most well-known for its teachings on meditation and mindfulness.

Secular practices of mindfulness have also entered mainstream culture. Jon Kabat-Zinn created Mindfulness-Based Stress Reduction (MBSR) programs at the University of Massachusetts Medical School over 35 years ago. Since then, many studies have documented health benefits of mindfulness and meditation. Now MBSR and other mindfulness programs are routinely offered in hospitals, schools, prisons, business leadership programs, and corporations.

Myths About Mindfulness

Many people are using the word *mindfulness* these days, often interchangeably with the word *meditation*, which can lead to confusion. There are also some common myths about mindfulness. Here are just a few:

- *Myth 1 **Mindfulness is the same thing as meditation.*** Formal meditation techniques can help develop concentration, clarity, emotional intelligence, and awareness of habitual thoughts, so we can direct them toward peaceful and wise states. While Buddhist meditation is one well-developed practice of mindfulness, through mindfulness we can bring awareness to the present moment in small ways no matter where we are or what we are doing. In other words, we don't need to meditate in order to practice mindfulness.

- *Myth 2 **If I am not happy and peaceful, I am doing it wrong.*** Sometimes mindfulness can bring more peace and joy, and other times it can bring up pain or grief we are avoiding. Like learning to walk as a child, mindfulness is a practice we stumble with at first and strengthen over time. We become more accepting of the thoughts, emotions, and bodily sensations we may be feeling at any moment, no matter how pleasant or unpleasant they may be.

- *Myth 3 Mindfulness means having no thoughts at all.* Many people think mindfulness is about having a quiet mind or being at war with our thoughts. We are not trying to ignore or block our thoughts. Instead, we notice them as we would notice a cloud passing in the sky. At times there may be patchy clouds that stay with us. Other times we can let them drift on their way and we can return to the present moment.

- *Myth 4 Mindfulness requires setting aside a lot of time.* You may think you have to set aside a large chunk of time or get a fancy meditation cushion to get started. While these are useful, they are not necessary for practicing mindfulness in small ways in your everyday life. We can be mindful in the grocery checkout line, as we drive to work, or as we eat a meal.

Basic Skills for Mindfulness

Bringing mindfulness into your life can start with simple practices. There are some basic skills and mindsets that can help you get started.

- *Noticing the present moment.* Much of our mental energies are focused on the past, the future, or how we wish things were. Putting this aside on occasion can help us break out of unhelpful thoughts and unconscious kneejerk reactions. Then we may be able to listen more deeply to another person, offer gratitude for the blessings in our lives, or work with the situation in front of us right now.

- *Staying grounded and in your body.* Have you ever tensed up during a conversation before you fully understood what was making you uncomfortable? Noticing physical reactions can direct our attention to what emotions and thoughts may be arising for us, and how we may be spiraling off into a story about what is happening. Keeping thoughts from spinning out of control can help us pause before reacting so we can respond mindfully.

- *Recognizing thoughts and emotions for what they are.* Our thoughts and emotions are valuable pieces of information, but they are not necessarily reflective of reality. Treating our thoughts as right and accurate—as the absolute truth—can lead us astray. Give room to acknowledge and honor the thoughts and emotions you are experiencing now, while acknowledging they are different from anyone else's.

- *Encouraging curiosity and a nonjudgmental attitude.* Many people have developed a strong inner critic that tries to control their thoughts and reactions. Although the inner critic comes from a place of wanting to protect and help, its voice is not always helpful. It can even cause unintentional harm. In mindfulness, we strive to bring an attitude of curiosity and nonjudgment about our thoughts and emotions. By creating this room, we can release the inner critic and open up to new possibilities.

When I first started to learn about mindfulness, I became aware of the critical and reactive voice in my head. I had a realization that this voice was keeping me from being happy and successful, and was negatively impacting my relationships.

Thich Nhat Hanh, a Buddhist monk, speaks about the negative and positive seeds we all have inside of us, and which ones we are choosing to water each day. There is also a famous parable about a man teaching his grandson the lesson of the two wolves that battle inside us. One is filled with anger, greed, arrogance, shame, and ego. The other is filled with peace, generosity, faith, humility, and empathy. When the grandson asks which wolf will win, the old man replies, "The one you feed."

I hope that the practices in this book will help you water the seeds and feed the wolf you most want to cultivate in your life. You don't need to set aside a long time to start practicing mindfulness. You can start with the next five minutes.

How to Use This Book

This book covers 10 areas in life where mindfulness may be useful. These are topics many people struggle with and look to navigate through using mindfulness. Each chapter contributor was invited because of their experience and skill in teaching mindfulness to beginners who are working on these issues.

This book is designed to let you jump from topic to topic. Each chapter opens with a brief overview about a particular issue and how mindfulness can help. It includes some general tips for applying mindfulness in your daily life and then ends with a few practice exercises. Each exercise takes just a few minutes and can be done in a variety of settings.

For each practice exercise, you'll find a brief introduction and clear, step-by-step instructions for trying it out. At the end are tips to help you overcome any common obstacles that may arise and suggestions for varying the practice in different settings and situations.

You may find that some exercises are applicable for additional areas of your life, and not just the chapter they are listed in. For example, the One-Minute Breath Meditation on page 30 can cultivate focus and attention, but it can also help you cope with stress or anger as well as foster more patience and joy. If you want to find a specific practice by name, you can refer to the Index of Mindfulness Practices on page 158.

There are many opportunities to be more present. For instance, if we are stuck in traffic, we can focus on patience. Other times, we can take a moment to stop and breathe mindfully to bring clarity to a situation. In the upcoming chapters, you will find many useful ways to practice mindfulness in your daily life. I am grateful for the teachers who agreed to write a chapter for this book. They are some of the best in the country, and between them, they have many years of training and experience in teaching mindfulness. May these practices open the door to more freedom and peace in your life. Enjoy!

The seduction of always doing can keep us from exercising the discipline that being *requires.*

—Jon Kabat-Zinn,
Author and founder of
Mindfulness-Based Stress Reduction

Mindfulness of the Body

One easy way to practice mindfulness is by noticing physical sensations experienced by your body. The body is always in the present moment, and we can tune into what we are sensing and feeling physically as a way to become more aware and mindful. You can do this anytime, anywhere, even while doing an activity like driving, walking, or eating. Just remember to keep a relaxed, nonjudgmental attitude about what physical sensations you notice.

STEP ONE

Take a moment to set your focus or intention for this practice. In this case, decide that you will try to stay in your body and to focus on physical sensations instead of thoughts or emotions.

STEP TWO

Take a deep breath and let the muscles in your body relax.

STEP THREE

Notice physical sensations that your body is experiencing as you go through this activity, like the air in your nostrils as you breathe or the sensation of your feet on the floor.

STEP FOUR

If thoughts pop into your mind, notice them without judgment, and then return your attention to your body's physical sensations.

STEP FIVE

Stay in your body for a few minutes, until you are ready to stop.

The Mindfulness of the Body practice is helpful for those times when you want to relax your body physically, such as at the office when your shoulders are feeling tight or at night when you're trying to fall asleep. I enjoy doing this when I need a break after sitting at my computer for several hours.

Your brain's job is to think, so you will probably have difficulty "staying in your body" the entire time. Even as you focus on your physical sensations, thoughts will come into your mind. This is normal. Just remember to return your attention to the present moment, over and over again. You may also notice places in your body that feel tense or painful. Try to "breathe into them" and see if the sensations change during the exercise.

You can practice checking in with your body for a moment or two throughout the day. You can see what you notice anywhere in your body or focus your attention on a particular area like your shoulders or your feet. There are smartphone apps that can help you remember to do this, or you can set a reminder bell or post notes around your home to remind you to take mindfulness breaks.

Sense and Savor Walk

The Sense and Savor Walk is an opportunity to slow down and enjoy a short five-minute walk to notice the beauty around you. Too often we rush through our day instead of stopping to smell the roses. Here, we challenge ourselves to step away from the frenetic pace of life and notice as many pleasurable things as possible. By using our senses, we practice being relaxed and engaged, rather than being lost in our thoughts.

STEP ONE

Find a place to walk outside. Take three deep breaths, and then begin walking slowly. Wander where you feel called and take your time.

STEP TWO

Notice as many beautiful and pleasurable things as you can. Perhaps it is the breeze on your cheek or the rustling of a tree. Enjoy noticing every detail.

STEP THREE

Engage all your senses. What are you drawn to touch or smell? What sounds capture your attention? If you feel drawn to a particular item, give it your full attention. Stay with it until you are ready to discover something new.

STEP FOUR

When you are ready, close the practice with three deep breaths. Notice how you feel and offer gratitude for the experience.

This activity is helpful when you are feeling anxious or need a brief break. You can go to a park or a forest, or take your lunch break outside your office building. You can also walk near your home or anyplace that feels safe. I love the smell of a neighbor's fragrant yellow roses as I walk down the street close to my home.

You may notice resistance to staying with something because a faster pace feels more familiar to you, or you want to take in as many things as possible. Consider that you are seeking quality of connection and not quantity. I often greet trees, feel the texture of their bark, and stop to pick up pebbles on the ground. Take the time to look deeper at what is in front of you, and engage your senses.

You can shorten this exercise by observing the outdoors from a window in your home or office. You can still focus your curiosity and attention even if you cannot engage all of your senses. For example, I recently spent some time watching a squirrel and a bird in a tree outside our living room window and noticed the changing colors of light as the sun set for the evening.

Affirmations on Belonging

This practice reminds us that we are part of a greater human family, and we all experience the suffering and joys that are part of the shared human experience. It also helps us recognize our inherent worth and the worth of others. The affirmations are adapted from a blessing by my teacher Jerry Tello.

STEP ONE

Find a quiet place where you will be comfortable talking aloud.

STEP TWO

Speak these words aloud slowly: "I am loved. I am a blessing. I am sacred just the way I am. I have dignity. I have wisdom and gifts for the whole." Repeat three times.

STEP THREE

Now visualize someone you love and say these words aloud: "You are loved. You are a blessing. You are sacred just the way you are. You have dignity. You have wisdom and gifts for the whole." Repeat three times.

STEP FOUR

Think of the many people experiencing suffering in the world and say these words aloud: "You are loved. You are a blessing. You are sacred just the way you are. You have dignity. You have wisdom and gifts for the whole." Repeat three times.

STEP FIVE

Close with a commitment to show kindness, later that day or the next, to someone you love and to a stranger you don't know.

If you find it difficult to say these words at first, start with the affirmation just for yourself, and allow the words to sink in over the course of several days. Do this even if you feel uncomfortable—it's okay to fake it until you make it.

If you are short on time, you can say each affirmation once instead of three times. You can also write the affirmations down and place them somewhere you can see them every day, like in your car or on your mirror. Then you can read them silently or aloud each day.

two

Regaining Focus and Concentration

Yingzhao Liu

is design director for international products at LinkedIn, and resides at a Zen center.

I hear so many people say, "It's all about balance." But a balanced life seems elusive, doesn't it? You may be concentrating on work or enjoying a conversation with a friend when your phone buzzes—and your mind is off, guessing the reason for the notification. Even when you're driving and there's real danger to moving your attention off the road, the urge to check your phone seems irresistible. We all know those moments!

The Challenge

Our world seems to have sped up in this era of information overload and it continues to accelerate. We live in a historically unique time of massive societal change and countless distractions, and may get overwhelmed by everything that pulls at our attention. We multitask, trying to get everything done, and we seem to have less patience. When faced with a moment of waiting, many turn to their smartphones, looking for something to busy themselves with.

When your attention is divided across multiple priorities or tasks, it is easy to feel stressed and overloaded. Negative emotions like fear, anger, or worry can make it harder to concentrate. Add the growing anxiety that results if you're not able to finish your work, and before you know it, you're caught in a negative feedback loop. Practicing mindfulness can help you avoid that trap and stay calm in the face of multiple distractions, allowing you to focus better, work more efficiently, and be more present to what's going on around you.

How Mindfulness Helps

Mindfulness strengthens our ability to stay focused and execute tasks one at a time, which research has shown to be more efficient and effective than multitasking. This also brings more enjoyment as well, creating a virtuous circle. In addition, mindfulness helps us see our own thoughts more clearly, making it easier to recognize when we're expending energy on pointless, energy-sucking distractions or avoidant behavior. By clearing out mental clutter, we learn to prioritize better, and we better conserve valuable energy required to tackle meaningful activities. We also learn how to spend less energy on avoiding things that make us uncomfortable and cultivate the strength to face them head on—a skill that enhances the building of a fulfilling life.

What You Can Do

First, have the intention to regain focus and concentration. How we experience each day is our responsibility—how we engage with those around us, social media, and the greater world is all up to us. Practicing mindfulness is part of what you can do. Here are a few principles:

- **Practice simplicity.** Try what I like to call *monotasking*—do one thing at a time and resist the temptation to multitask. Remove "noise" from your life. For example, sign on to Do Not Call and Do Not Mail lists to reduce solicitations (see Resources on page 149), and if a source of media no longer satisfies, stop checking or unsubscribe. Notice if you habitually consume content that is no longer helpful. Donate or recycle unneeded possessions.

- **Try meditation.** We spend much time studying and understanding subjects, yet we generally don't study our minds. Meditation is this study. The mind has so much to do with our happiness, or lack thereof—so time spent understanding our own mind is extremely well spent. A one-minute breath meditation is introduced next to get you started. Look for meditation resources in your community and try a consistent practice for a few weeks.

- **Focus on the people in your world.** Mother Teresa said, "Let no one ever come to you without leaving better." Your full attention is a gift, and when you give it, you receive more than you give. Enlist family and friends in your intention. Good conversations with friends are some of life's most precious moments, so be mindful of distractions—you can place smartphones on the table when dining out, and whoever picks up their phone first pays the bill!

Change happens in subtle and unsubtle ways; you might not notice anything for a while, and then suddenly, you feel different—less divided or distracted. The following simple practices can help you live a more integrated life. Try them over a few weeks, and I would be very surprised if you don't see positive change unfolding!

One-Minute Breath Meditation

Our breath is always with us, yet very rarely noticed. It is a great tool for training our mind to focus and is a common door into other meditation techniques. Anyone can meditate; it's nothing mysterious. One minute of paying attention can shift you from a busy, overwhelmed moment to a feeling of presence and possibility.

STEP ONE

Begin by noticing your breath. Notice the sensation of the air around your nostrils and your upper lip, and notice the air moving in and out of your body, the rise and fall of your chest and abdomen. Breathe as you normally do, just with awareness.

STEP TWO

Start counting your breath: the first breath in and out is 1, the next in and out is 2, and continue on until 10. Ten breaths will take you close to one minute—then you're done!

This is a great practice you can do anywhere—in the checkout line at the grocery store, waiting for your kids to get out the door, or before starting a meeting, really any minute of the day. When you don't have one minute, do just one conscious breath. As author and spiritual thinker Eckhart Tolle has said, "One conscious breath is enough to make some space where before there was the uninterrupted succession of one thought after another. One conscious breath (two or three would be even better), taken many times a day, is an excellent way of bringing space into your life."

If you find yourself distracted before you get to 10, no problem. Don't judge yourself, and just come back to the counting. Compassion and patience for yourself is part of this practice!

If you have extra time, do the same breathing meditation for 10 minutes, sitting in a comfortable position. No matter how your day is going, this is 10 minutes of calm and quiet you can give yourself. Enjoy it.

Staying Present for a "Boring" Task

Life contains a lot of mundane tasks: washing dishes and folding laundry are common examples. We can also expend a great deal of energy avoiding some of these tasks, which can create feelings of guilt, shame, or dread, at the expense of our peace of mind. Instead of avoidance, or doing them in a distracted way and wishing we didn't have to, we can see these tasks as great opportunities for mindfulness practice.

STEP ONE

Take a few deep breaths in and out, with intentional thoughts of completing your task mindfully.

STEP TWO

Now begin your task. Notice the physical sensations you are experiencing. Notice the texture and temperature of touch, as well as the movement of your hands and your body. For example, if you are washing dishes, you might notice the temperature of the water, the way the sponge feels in your hand, or the weight or texture of the various items you are washing.

STEP THREE

As you continue to note the rich sensations that have often escaped your awareness—enjoy them. Allow the sensations to become a source of pleasure and focus for you in this moment. If you notice your mind wandering, take a deep breath and return to noticing physical sensations.

STEP FOUR

Close with a deep breath offering gratitude to yourself for completing the task.

You have the choice to be present in any routine task, which takes up so much of our lives. Be curious about your experience of physically being in the world, the way young children do—and the world becomes magical, as it is for them.

The mind has a tendency to distract us so we are not present. You may also notice common reactions like negative thoughts about the task, rushing to get it over with, frustrations you feel. Or you may notice physical discomfort while doing the task. Just notice these sensations without judgment. The key is to gently bring your awareness back to the physical sensations when it wanders from the task at hand.

If you have more time, note what default thoughts you might want to experiment with changing next time. Perhaps shift from "I hate doing this!" to "How can I be a master in this activity?" or "How will completing this task benefit me and others?" You can also reflect on what you noticed that could provide ideas for making the task less effortful and more enjoyable.

Understanding the
Parts and the Whole

When negative emotions like frustration, anger, or anxiety arise, it is easy to become so caught up in the feelings that you can't focus or concentrate on what is in front of you—whether that's work, a routine task, a conversation, or even the road. You've temporarily lost your center, your sense of wholeness. Taking a few moments to acknowledge that what you are feeling is not who you are shifts your perspective and grounds you, allowing you to be fully present for the challenge of the moment.

STEP ONE

When you feel an uncomfortable emotion such as frustration, say to yourself, "A part of me is really frustrated," rather than "I am really frustrated." You can say this silently if you're in the presence of others. See that you have this part of you that's frustrated, rather than you are this part. Other parts of you may be patient, relieved, or any number of possibilities.

STEP TWO

Shift your posture to have both feet on the floor, spine straight, chest more open, chin level, and eyes looking farther out. We do these adjustments often unconsciously when centering is needed—your body knows what to do.

STEP THREE

Acknowledge that the part that is frustrated is present, without judging it or wanting it to go away. Often this allows the emotion to soften a bit, and a shift begins to take place.

This practice can be done anywhere, and without adding extra time to whatever you're doing. It does have the effect of adding a little space where there didn't seem to be any.

Too much focus on the negative emotions is a common obstacle. Seeing yourself as parts of the whole allows you to see the habitual patterns in your life—getting frustrated or angry, checking out, or anything else—with fresh eyes. When you see these patterns, acknowledge their usefulness in your life—they've protected you from pain—but don't become them. This is the work of understanding the parts and the whole. Over time, as these parts have less control over you, you will have a greater range of possible responses in any given situation. This is mindfulness in action.

If time permits, try this variation: In addition to saying to yourself, "A part of me is frustrated (or angry or some other negative emotion)," physically ground and center yourself as described in step 2, and become curious about what is happening inside. The part may want to tell you something, or other parts may voice judgment for the first part. Each time you do this, you will learn something about yourself—how your mind works. This is not a once or twice type of practice, but an ongoing practice. We have the rest of our lives to learn about ourselves, right? Practices like this are tools for happiness, and they are in your hands now.

three

Cultivating Gratitude and Joy

Kaira Jewel Lingo

teaches mindfulness in the United States and internationally to general audiences, as well as educators, families, activists, and artists. She is inspired by the power of mindfulness to foster community, healing, and justice.

You're standing at the checkout line in the grocery store looking through the latest magazine. Seeing page after page of youthful bodies, unhappiness and insecurity about your own creeps into your awareness. When you get home, you check your Facebook feed. As you compare your own accomplishments to those of your friends and acquaintances, more feelings of inferiority and not-being-good-enough arise. Soon you are ruminating on all the things you don't like about yourself, and your mood sinks even lower. Due to the hard wiring of the brain and social conditioning, we tend to focus on negative aspects of our lives, often becoming chronically unhappy. It doesn't have to be that way. With mindfulness, we can take control of our reactions to thoughts, and make joy and gratitude a daily practice.

Happiness Is Here and Now

In a culture of instant gratification, it's ironic that many of us sacrifice the joy and goodness available to us right now by straining to get something else that we think we need. Often we put off happiness in the moment, believing we can only be happy once we get a new car, earn a higher degree, or find the right partner. But happiness is available to us right here and now. It does not have to be an idealized future. As radical as it may sound, the present moment is the only place we can truly touch happiness. The present moment is the only moment we have—the past is gone, and the future is not yet here. We can stop our constant searching for something else to make us happy and instead look closely at what is right in front of us.

Here is a personal example of how mindfulness can bring us joy: When my dad turned 68, I decided to write him 68 thank-yous. At first, I thought it would be difficult to come up with 68 things. But as I began to reflect on the many things he had done for me, the seed of gratitude in me grew stronger and stronger, and I eventually wrote down 90 all together; more still come to me from time to time. Here are just a few of the things I thanked my dad for:

Changing my diapers as a baby and doing my hair as a child; listening deeply to many people who need support and care in your counseling work and your everyday life; the interest you show in people you meet every day; the encouragement you give to waiters, taxi drivers, rental car folks, airline customer service representatives, neighbors, etc.; fixing delicious tomato soup whenever I would get sick as a child; and giving me the space to choose what college to attend and refusing to give me your opinion so I wouldn't be influenced (even when I chose the school that was farthest from you).

After I wrote down these expressions of gratitude (my "gratitudes"), my happiness was so great! Nothing external had changed—I wasn't any wealthier, I didn't have more friends, and I didn't have more knowledge. I just came to appreciate more deeply what I had been taking for granted most of my life. And of course, when I gave the letter to my father, he was also very happy. He told me he takes my letter with him everywhere he goes and when he's not feeling so good about himself, he reads it and feels better. So with the letter, I made both of us happy. And, of course, his happiness increased my own happiness.

I've shared this practice with many people, and I constantly hear from people who tell me they've written such a letter of appreciation to a loved one. They always tell me what a difference it has made in their relationship and how glad they are to know this practice. I encourage you to try it for yourself by writing down the things you appreciate about a person and then giving it to them. You may be surprised by how good it makes you feel.

How Mindfulness Helps

Mindfulness helps us generate joy and gratitude from within rather than waiting for outer circumstances to make us happy. The kind of happiness we generate through awareness is more fulfilling and lasts longer than the satisfaction we get from consuming things. Research has shown that those who regularly practice awareness of gratitude have lower blood pressure and cholesterol levels, sleep better and wake up feeling more refreshed, have fewer conflicts in relationships, and experience higher life satisfaction.

Mindfulness helps us dwell fully in the present moment and not get caught in the past or the future. It is only when we are aware of ourselves and our actions that we can touch the richness and beauty already in our lives. This is because our brains have what researchers term a *negativity bias*. This means we focus more on the things that are going wrong than the things that are going well. Research shows that negative experiences are immediately stored in long-term memory, whereas it takes positive experiences 12 to 20 seconds to be stored in long-term memory.

According to Barbara Fredrickson, a psychology professor at the University of Michigan, our positive emotions are more subtle compared to the intensity of our negative emotions. Mindfulness helps us to be aware of a positive experience when it is arising, which strengthens the experience and our *very capacity* to be happy. The more aware we are of the good things in our lives, the more we tend to notice them. This way, we slowly begin to alter our inherent negativity bias so we can be more nourished by the positive things in our lives.

With mindfulness, we can be aware that the sun is there, the earth is there, we have oxygen to breathe, and that we can breathe in and out. If our lungs, eyes, skin, and digestive system are functioning, we appreciate these gifts of health because we know that for many people this is not the case. Even in times of loss, illness, and life challenges, we can experience gratitude, and this will give us more stability and peace to go through our difficulties.

There are many conditions for happiness or gratitude already available to us. We must be present to notice them. The potential for joy and gratitude is always there in us, even if it is dormant, and if we are mindful, we will remember to wake up these qualities and make them arise in our minds.

What You Can Do

* ***Smiling.*** As soon as you wake up in the morning, be aware of your breath and your body; feel your aliveness. Don't get out of bed straightaway. Practice smiling. If it helps, think of it as mouth yoga. Smiling helps all the muscles in your face relax. University of Kansas psychologists, Sarah Pressman and Tara Kraft, found that smiling reduces stress. Other studies have shown that smiling, even if it is not spontaneously brought on by good feelings, activates "feel-good" chemicals in the brain that can elevate your mood.

   If you can smile first thing in the morning, you start a good habit that's easier to continue throughout the day. You can smile to the fact that you are still alive; another day is available to you, and that's a real gift! Try using the following verse by Thich Nhat Hanh to remind you, and post it near your bed so you see it as soon as you wake up:

Waking up this morning, I smile
Twenty-four brand new hours are all for me
I am determined to live them mindfully
And look at everyone with eyes of compassion and love

- *Catching neutral moments.* As you move through your day, notice the moments when you are neither happy nor upset, the neutral moments, where things are just okay. We usually only notice the moments when we are feeling really good or very low. Instead, try to notice the in-between states. These neutral states often lead to boredom and more negative mental states if we aren't paying attention. This is because neutral states tend to narrow our mindsets, whereas positive states widen our mindset and help us connect to others, according to Barbara Fredrickson. Catch the neutral moments and purposely bring up joy and gratitude. So if you are stuck in traffic or in between appointments, use the time to remember something that happened recently that made you happy or grateful. It can be as small as gratitude for the elevator working or the sound of birds singing outside your window.

- *Make a list of things that make you happy.* You can continue to proactively cultivate joy by making a list of the things you do that make you happy. Perhaps it's exercising, singing, going to a museum, writing, fixing things around the house, helping others, or bringing beauty to an area of your home. Post your list where you will see it every day and make sure you do at least one of these things each day.

- *Give up complaining.* The practice of not complaining and not focusing on what we dislike is as important as actively cultivating our joy. Try taking a day or a week to pay particular attention to moments or situations when you tend to complain—either inwardly or verbalized to others. Complaining is an attitude of staying stuck in a negative situation, which just makes it worse. Refraining from complaining doesn't mean bottling up or suppressing difficult feelings. If something is wrong, it's important to speak about it in a way that leads to a helpful solution. But often, we repeat and rehearse over and over our dislike of something without any intention to act constructively. This only increases our unhappiness. Make a commitment to give up complaining for a determined period of time. You can let someone else know you are doing this practice to help you stay on track.

Remember, just like mindfulness, joy and gratitude are like muscles. The more we utilize them, the stronger they become and the easier it is to access them. I have become a happier person through the practice of mindfulness. I know many people who have also been able to touch deeper joy and gratitude—even in the midst of big life challenges—thanks to mindfulness. Watch the videos listed in the Resources on page 149. There is scientific evidence that the power of mindfulness and the daily practice of joy and gratitude rewire the brain to become happier and healthier.

Whatever we water grows. And it's up to us to choose what seeds we are watering in the garden of our minds. If you fall back into negative thinking, try not to judge yourself, but just begin again as soon as you remember. The following three exercises will help you grow and strengthen your gratitude and joy muscles. Enjoy!

Sometimes your joy is the source of your smile, but sometimes your smile can be the source of your joy.

—Thich Nhat Hanh,
Author and Buddhist monk

Three Gratitudes

You can take time every day to be aware of three things you are grateful for. This powerful practice can teach you to look for the good that is always around us. It can be a real game changer. As the 13th-century theologian Meister Eckhart said, "If the only prayer you ever said in your whole life was 'thank you,' that would be enough."

STEP ONE

Settle yourself in a comfortable sitting or lying posture. Be aware of your breathing. Allow your body to rest and release tension.

STEP TWO

Bring to mind something you feel grateful for. Think of it in as much detail as you can.

STEP THREE

Be aware of where in your body you feel this gratitude. Be aware of any other emotions that arise with the feeling of gratitude.

STEP FOUR

Hold this awareness of gratitude in your mind for 12 to 20 seconds (remember, this is how long it takes positive memories to lodge in long-term memory, whereas negative memories get lodged immediately).

STEP FIVE

Bring to mind two more things you feel grateful for, repeating steps 3 and 4 for each one.

Try writing your gratitudes at the beginning or end of the day. At the start of a meal, be aware of three things you are grateful for. This practice is also a great way to end a trip, meeting, or other event. You can reflect on your own or invite others who participated with you to also express their gratitude. You can also invite a friend to exchange gratitudes with you by e-mail or text each day.

When we are in a low mood or upset, it is difficult to remember to be grateful. But it is exactly in these moments that gratitude can uplift us and change our state of mind. Especially if we make it a habit when times are good, it will be easier to do in challenging moments.

If you are short on time, you can use moments of transition to practice your gratitudes—riding up the elevator, walking to your car, or walking to the bathroom. If you have more time, this could also be a refreshing way to start a meeting or gathering, inviting everyone to reflect on three gratitudes, possibly in pairs or with the whole group.

Expressing Appreciation

Expressing appreciation is a powerful way to cultivate joy and gratitude and transform our inherent negativity bias. It can be as simple as appreciating someone's smile or expressing our happiness that they are in good health.

STEP ONE

Settle yourself in a comfortable sitting or lying posture. Be aware of your breathing. Allow your body to rest and release tension.

STEP TWO

Bring to mind a person in your life you wish to appreciate. Reflect on this person's good qualities, how they have been helpful or kind to you or others, or how they live with integrity and respect.

STEP THREE

Be aware of how reflecting on this person's goodness affects your body and mind.

STEP FOUR

Express your appreciation to this person verbally or in writing as soon as you are able to.

This can be a very powerful practice to do regularly with family members and friends. You could make it a habit to express your appreciation to each other on a weekly basis. Sit together on a predetermined night each week, perhaps over a meal, and each take turns expressing something you appreciate about each other.

This practice can feel awkward at first. It's important to express only what we sincerely feel, as this is not flattery. If you can't think of much to appreciate, there may be some hurt or resentment in your heart. It is important to address this at the appropriate time. The appreciation practice isn't about sweeping things under the rug and suppressing them. But even when you are hurt by someone, being aware of that person's good qualities can help you see the bigger picture and not be overly focused on what you perceive is wrong with them.

You can practice an abbreviated form of this practice by expressing appreciation to people you encounter briefly throughout the day thanking the checkout clerk at the grocery store, smiling at the restaurant server, or wishing the bus driver a good day.

A Random Act of Kindness

A powerful way to increase your joy and gratitude is to do something kind for others, especially without any expectation or wish that the act be reciprocated. While happiness can come from many things, the deepest and longest-lasting happiness comes from helping someone else. You can make it a habit to do an act of kindness each day.

STEP ONE

Settle yourself in a comfortable sitting or lying posture. Be aware of your breathing. Allow your body to rest and release tension.

STEP TWO

Reflect on how you can reach out to help someone in your life today and perform a random act of kindness.

STEP THREE

Visualize yourself doing this act of kindness.

STEP FOUR

Notice how contemplating this makes you feel in your body and mind.

STEP FIVE

Do this act of kindness as soon as you are able. If you are busy, write the idea down and put it somewhere you will see it so you remember to act on it later.

Be on the lookout as you go through your day for ways to help others. There may be someone who gives you a surprise opportunity to practice kindness—a relative you haven't heard from in a while who calls and needs some attention, a homeless person you cross paths with, or someone stressed at work who really needs a kind word or assistance.

Sometimes we second-guess our first and natural impulse to help others. We feel afraid or shy, or we worry that our help will not be wanted. Or we feel we can't actually afford to give what we are initially inspired to. We can practice trusting our first instinct and make it a habit to just give or help, to not let our fear or worries stymie our natural generosity and openheartedness. This allows our heart to grow bigger. Often when we open to give and share with others, we notice more comes back to us.

If you have time, it may be helpful to write down your experiences of expressing kindness. Whenever we stop to reflect on and write about our joy and gratitude, they grow. Our capacity to feel joy and gratitude is strengthened. Share your experiences of kindness with your friends to nurture gratitude and joy in them as well. You can even have a buddy with whom you regularly exchange experiences of your random acts of kindness. Try doing a week- or month-long practice with someone else and share your stories with each other every day.

four

Promoting Patience and Compassion

Jacoby Ballard

has been practicing yoga and Buddhism for 20 years and cofounded Third Root Community Health Center, in Brooklyn, New York, to help people of all backgrounds have better access to yoga, acupuncture, herbal medicine, and other healing services.

T hich Nhat Hanh, a Buddhist monk, says, "It is easy to tell how happy someone is by observing how compassionate she is toward others." We all strive to be happy and hope that our actions reflect this inner state of well-being; yet at times, being patient and compassionate may be some of the hardest things to do.

It may be difficult to be compassionate with a family member who is always late, struggling in life, or falling behind in school. Or perhaps we lose our patience with a noisy neighbor, a rude coworker, or even with a computer that just crashed. Or perhaps you are the speedy driver becoming impatient with the slow driver ahead.

The good news is that patience and compassion are like muscles. As we begin to practice them, they strengthen.

The Challenge

As a co-founder at Third Root Community Health Center, I often scheduled the activities in our space. Sometimes, a yoga teacher would be late or not show up at all. I would get mad and reprimand them. My thoughts automatically went to judging them, thinking about how irresponsible they were.

The truth is, life will not always go as we planned or how we would like it. That is true for us as well as for others. Stress, difficulty, and challenges are inevitable in this life. What you or others are currently facing could be as insignificant as a late bus, as profound as a recent death in the family, or even the prolonged impacts of social injustice in the world.

It is common to want to avoid suffering in our life by pretending to be in control, being in denial, withdrawing, retaliating in anger, or placing the blame on ourselves or on others. When we are feeling stressed, we might judge ourselves and think, "Why can't I do this right? I'm a screw-up!"

Thus, we suffer from the original experience, and we suffer more from our thoughts and judgments about our experience. In our hurt or disappointment, we may retaliate, which may create more suffering and harm our relationships.

How Mindfulness Helps

When we find ourselves getting impatient or judgmental, mindfulness can help us shift our attention to get curious about what is happening. Faced with hurt, pain, or disappointment, we can shut down and turn away, or open our hearts even broader. Before, we might demand, "Why did this happen to me?" but with compassion and patience, we might say, "How could this happen and how can we resolve it?"

With the yoga teachers who were late, I eventually learned that each one of them wanted to be effective and good at their job. In most cases, whatever caused them to be late was not something they chose.

Because of my mindfulness practice, I shifted from asking, "What's wrong with you?" to asking, "Are you okay? What's going on? Is there anything I can help you with?"

Through practicing compassion, we literally change the structure of our brains that, by instinct, propel us away from what is perceived as negative or threatening, toward pleasure. Patience grows our ability to tolerate pain and discomfort, and the strength to respond skillfully in uncomfortable situations. Compassion for ourselves and for others allows us to trust in the innate goodness of all beings and show empathy—that we are human and make mistakes. We can relate to the experience of being human, struggling to do better. When we realize our experiences help us learn and grow, we can have more compassion for ourselves and for others when things are not what we wanted or expected.

What You Can Do

The day after I moved to Brooklyn, I was rolling my cart down the street. A woman shouted several expletives at me as I went by, and I realized I must have run over her toes with my cart. I also knew the neighborhood demographics were changing rapidly, causing worry for those who had lived there a long time and mistrust of the strangers moving in.

A week later, I saw her and said, "I'm so sorry I hurt you last week." She replied, "No big deal." I said, "Given what you said to me, it did seem like it was a big deal, and I want you to know that I would never do anything to intentionally hurt you. I respect you and I respect this neighborhood." I saw part of her armor soften, her shoulders lower, and her jaw relax. It reminded me of a yoga teacher, Seane Corn, who had once remarked that more patience and compassion is needed in our neighborhoods.

Pain and discomfort are inevitable, but prolonged suffering is optional. Whether it was the teachers who were late or the woman I apologized to, I had a choice. I could harbor resentment and shame, or avoid them, escalating the situation and adding to my suffering and the suffering of others. When we aspire to extend patience and compassion instead, we heal some of our suffering and the suffering in the world.

Compassion and self-care for ourselves when we feel pain or are overwhelmed also helps us cope with the frustration and suffering we see in the world. Self-compassion helps us be more calm and spacious when life inevitably throws us unexpected disappointments and surprises.

Our external circumstances are all opportunities to practice patience and compassion, and we develop this capacity through our practice. When we feel impatience or judgment, we can ask ourselves, "What is going to improve this moment? What can I say or do that can ease suffering? Perhaps I cannot make it completely better, but I can do one small thing. How can I acknowledge my own feelings while also showing patience, empathy, or understanding right now?"

Before learning about mindfulness, I would have yelled at unsafe drivers on the road without wondering if they might have their own reasons for speeding, perhaps an urgent need to get to the hospital or worry about missing an important appointment. While I might not agree with their behavior, I find I have choices in how I react. I can get out of their way and offer a blessing that they and everyone around them arrive safely at their destinations.

Cultivating patience and compassion can help us nourish our family relationships, collaborate with our coworkers, and extend kindness in the world, even to strangers. By releasing our rigid expectations, we can release some of our suffering and meet the moment and other people exactly as they are.

It is tremendously liberating when you don't take things so personally.

— Jack Kornfield,
Author and Buddhist teacher

Giving and Receiving Patience

This exercise focuses your attention on cultivating patience for yourself and others. Set aside a few minutes to focus on patience when you can do so without interruption or becoming overwhelmed.

STEP ONE

Sit in a comfortable position, lowering your gaze or closing your eyes.

STEP TWO

Breathe deeply a few times. When your attention is steady, repeat these words in your mind with each breath: "Breathing in, I breathe love for myself. Breathing out, I breathe patience for myself." We begin with ourselves so that we can extend that same kindness to others later. Do this for one minute.

STEP THREE

Now think of someone you are happy with. As you think of them, repeat these words in your mind with each breath: "Breathing in, I breathe love for you. Breathing out, I breathe patience for you." Do this for one minute.

STEP FOUR

Now think of someone you are struggling to be patient with. As you think of them, repeat these words in your mind with each breath: "Breathing in, I breathe love for you. Breathing out, I breathe patience for you." Do this for one minute.

STEP FIVE

Finally, take three breaths, repeating these thoughts in your mind: "Breathing in, I am an embodiment of love. Breathing out, I am an embodiment of patience." Go about your day.

If you find yourself distracted, don't become impatient or judge yourself. Just come back to the expressions when you notice a distraction. Compassion and patience for yourself is part of this practice!

If you have extra time, do steps 2–4 for two or three minutes each for a longer exercise. If you are pressed for time, repeat steps 2–4 for only three breaths each instead of one minute, or focus your time just on step 5.

Meeting Pain with Compassion

This practice is useful to connect with compassion around suffering. Begin by working with situations that caused discomfort for you, but are not overwhelming. Perhaps someone was impatient with you or said something that had a negative impact on you.

STEP ONE

Allow yourself to recall a moment of suffering that touched your life, where there were unkind words or actions. Feel the difficult situation in your body (how you physically react), and notice the way you breathe as you remember.

STEP TWO

As you hold this situation in your heart, repeat these phrases: "This is a moment of suffering. Suffering is a part of life. May I turn toward this unwanted situation with compassion, and allow it to broaden my heart and deepen my practice."

STEP THREE

Think of someone you know who is suffering, perhaps because you offered unkind words or actions to them. Feel the difficult situation in your body, and notice the way you breathe as you remember.

STEP FOUR

As you hold this situation in your heart, repeat these phrases: "This is a moment of suffering. Suffering is a part of life. May I turn toward this unwanted situation with compassion, and allow it to broaden my heart and deepen my practice."

STEP FIVE

Close with a few final breaths, recognizing that we are all capable of causing suffering and receiving suffering, and that we are all capable of causing happiness and receiving happiness. Go about your day.

If you become overwhelmed, it can be useful to simply open your eyes, and notice three unique things about the space you are sitting in, feel your feet on the ground, and notice your breath. This will help you reorient and remember that you are no longer in that difficult situation, and that you are safe now and can work to heal the pain of the past.

If you feel comfortable and safe doing so, consider talking with the person who came to mind. Share that you would like to practice offering and receiving compassionate words and actions, and ask for their support in doing so.

Sending Silent Waves
of Compassion

Over time, the aspiration is to welcome every being into our hearts. Out of compassion for ourselves, we start with those just around us, so we can cultivate the muscle of compassion in our everyday life. At first it may seem strange, but over time you will feel more compassionate toward yourself and others in the world. You can do this exercise while riding the bus, at work, or in your home while sitting with your family having a meal.

STEP ONE

Take a deep breath. Then as you continue to breathe in and out, soften your gaze and look down while you repeat these words in your mind: "May I be safe from danger. May my pain be held in compassion." Continue this for one minute.

STEP TWO

Now notice those around you. Choose one person you would like to extend compassion to. As you breathe in and out, soften your gaze and look down while you repeat these words in your mind: "May you be safe from danger. May your pain be held in compassion." Continue this for one minute.

STEP THREE

Next, choose one person you perhaps are less inclined to extend compassion to, either because of recent experiences you have had with them, or because they are very different from you, or you sense some judgment you have about them even though you don't know them. As you breathe in and out, soften your gaze and look down while you repeat these words in your mind: "May you be safe from danger. May your pain be held in compassion." Continue this for one minute.

STEP FOUR

Close your exercise with a final breath with the following thought: "May all beings be safe from danger. May all beings' pain be held in compassion." Go about your day.

Scientific research has shown that practicing loving-kindness meditation, from which this Sending Silent Waves of Compassion is derived, has numerous health benefits. A landmark study by Barbara Frederickson showed that seven weeks of loving-kindness meditation increased positive emotions like love and joy and decreased depressive symptoms. Other studies have demonstrated effects of reducing chronic pain, migraine pain, and symptoms of PTSD.

five

Dealing with Stress and Worry

Acharya Gaylon Ferguson

is an associate professor in Interdisciplinary Studies at Naropa University and the author of two books: Natural Wakefulness: Discovering the Wisdom We Were Born With *and* Natural Bravery: Fear and Fearlessness as a Direct Path to Awakening.

F ive years ago this summer, I wrote in my journal:

"This morning I awoke feeling stressed out again. Lately it's been happening more and more frequently. Mounting pressures at work are directly followed by increasing tensions at home—concerns about the health of my family, arguments about money and financial uncertainties, wrestling with our schedules to find good quality time to be together. As the old saying goes: What is wrong with this picture?"

It is likely we all have had similar feelings. Mindfulness can help us find relief from anxiety and stress, as well as the mounting challenges of life in general.

A Pervasive Challenge

Stress is defined as "mental or emotional strain or tension resulting from very demanding circumstances." This sounds like a description of modern life. Given the economic, political, environmental, social, racial, and gender challenges of our times, who does not feel that we are living in "demanding circumstances?" We are not alone in feeling this strain or tension—even if the responsibility for meeting this challenge in *our* lives falls primarily to us. Mindfulness arose as an insightful response to our common human condition—which now includes the tension of facing our demanding circumstances.

Many psychologists describe our society as fast becoming a "culture of fear." This is not just an abstract, social scientific description, but something most of us feel part of every day. Is this water safe for our children to drink? Will I lose my job because of downsizing or shifts in the global economy? What about these additives in our food? What about global terrorism and violence and brutality in our neighborhoods? What about the rise in addictions and trauma? We are all very concerned about "what might happen."

How Mindfulness Helps

First of all, mindfulness teaches us that fear and large challenges in our everyday life are normal; they are not signs that we are doing something wrong. Here, I want to offer you the opposite suggestion—that our concern about ourselves, our families, our communities is a *good* sign, a sign of life surging up in us. Yes, we care about our lives at home, at work, in our neighborhoods. Some of the stress and worry we feel arises directly from this caring.

If we did not care, we would just calmly sail right through every day like a person who is numb to what is going on around her. When we go to the dentist, sometimes we need to take a temporary anesthetic to numb us so that we will not feel the pain of the dental work being done. But living a life permanently numbed to what's happening to us and to the ones we love is not really what we want. As long as we are alive, we will feel. As long as we feel, we will care. As long as we care, we will feel concern. Such concern goes hand in hand with our ability to love. No love, no caring. The more love, the more caring and feeling and concern. Is this true in your life today? It's certainly true in mine.

So mindfulness helps, first of all, by giving us another view—an approach to our feelings and experience that does not begin with the deficit model, that there is something basically wrong with us that is causing us to feel what we feel. Instead, mindfulness helps us regard even our sense of strain as a good sign, as felt personal evidence of our fundamental human caring. Rather than beginning with the oppressive view that we are basically defective, mindfulness helps us celebrate being human.

What You Can Do

Last spring, I met someone in Washington, D.C., whose close friend had just suffered a miscarriage; she was understandably sad about this loss. This person came to me for meditation instruction in the practice of mindfulness, wanting to know how long it was appropriate to grieve such a loss. Honestly, I do not know. I do not trust sources that tell us how many weeks the human heart can be allowed to fully and properly "process" grief. Instead, I am learning and relearning to trust what my Southern, African-American grandmother called "mother wit"—that each person has an innate sense of how long she needs to grieve, when she is ready to laugh and dance again. Mindfulness for some of us is a way of returning to trust this inner knowing, this intuitive wisdom of the heart. Mindfulness is cultivating what has recently been called "emotional intelligence" (I like to call it "mother wit").

Emotional intelligence and trust in our intuitive wisdom and compassion can be helpful in releasing us into this vivid, heartbreaking, challenging journey we call "life." We have to make the hard choice to feel our feelings, rather than take the easier course and become numb when presented with stressful situations. When we practice mindfulness and explore our feelings, we are more alive and present, engaged, and able to move. Numbing ourselves, in contrast, is a short-term solution that can eventually lead to despair and the feeling of being stuck or victimized by what's happening around us.

Mindfulness helps us recognize this need to be fully present, rather than ignore or retreat from reality. It is not an opiate for putting up with interpersonal and social conditions while hoping they will go away. When we feel our own feelings and feel our sense perceptions, we also reconnect with nature: the earth and the sky, the wind and the rain. These are our allies for "waking up" to the world as it is and seeing reality clearly. From here, we can engage our lives to bring about positive change—in our communities, the earth, and ourselves. Mindfulness actually empowers us so that we're more engaged and able to transform, creating inner and outer change together.

Fear is the cheapest room in the house. I would like to see you living in better conditions.

—Hafiz, 14th century Persian poet

Mindfulness of Bare Attention

This simple exercise helps you become more aware of the difference between the direct experience of doing something and the thoughts you have about that experience. Learning to discern this difference may not seem important at first, but we need this skill to create space between our direct experiences and the perceptions we have of these experiences. For example, many people have a fear of public speaking, not because the act of speaking in front of others is painful, but because the stories they have around the experience create fear or anxiety. The first step in freeing ourselves from these stories, then, is learning to recognize them.

STEP ONE

The next time you sit down for a delicious meal, take a morsel of food and look at it. Examine it, smell it, touch it, and feel it.

STEP TWO

Close your eyes and taste this piece of food. Begin chewing it slowly, savoring the juices and texture. Recognize that you are experiencing a direct experience; tasting the food directly is called "bare attention," or mindfulness of eating.

STEP THREE

When you finish eating this piece, close your eyes and think about the food—remember its color and flavor. Simply take a moment to notice the difference between the memory of eating and the direct experience of actually eating that piece of food.

STEP FOUR

With the next taste, repeat step 2, and continue eating while directly feeling, sensing, and tasting the food. Notice the contrast between this direct experience and the "memory" you have just recalled.

You can try this practice with any simple activity that involves your physical senses. Start by noticing the physical sensations involved in the activity, whether it is petting your cat's soft fur and listening to its purrs, or feeling the warmth of soapy water as you wash slippery dishes. Just remember to add the final step of closing your eyes when you are finished and noticing the contrast between physically feeling these sensations and simply thinking about them. Can you see how what you just experienced is separate from your thoughts about that experience?

Mindfulness of Feeling

While thoughts about experiences are important, mindfulness of feelings matters, too. Part of this practice is directly feeling any emotions the moment they arise in your body, including fear, sadness, anger, worry, or being overwhelmed. When you choose an emotion to recall for this practice exercise (the example given here is fear), pick one that is moderate in intensity, something that might register a 4 or 5 on a scale where 1 is barely noticeable and 10 is overwhelmingly strong. Set aside time for this activity when you are free to focus on yourself.

STEP ONE

Get comfortable, and take a few deep breaths. Let yourself relax your body.

STEP TWO

Bring up the memory of a familiar fear and then feel the emotion in your body. Take a moment to notice your physical reactions to the fear with curiosity and gentleness. What sensations are coming up that we might call "fear?" When you are afraid, how does your body really feel? Is it an energy in the body? A constricted feeling in your throat or stomach? A suddenly quickening pulse? Rapidly alternating thoughts of flight or fight?

STEP THREE

Try not to pay attention to the stories you tell yourself about why you feel afraid or the cause of your feelings. The idea is to try to avoid thinking about the concepts and ideas we all have about "negative" emotions.

STEP FOUR

You may notice that it's hard to stay focused on the physical sensations of your fear. What thoughts keep popping up? How does your body react? Simply notice them, and then return to focusing on the physical sensation of the emotion itself.

STEP FIVE

After a few moments, take a few more deep breaths and then end the practice.

Mindfulness of fear means staying with the moment-to-moment embodied experience of feeling afraid. It means experiencing this sensation without judging it or trying to push it away: "What's wrong with me that I'm feeling this again? I thought I worked through this already!" At the same time, mindfulness of emotions means not acting them out right away or justifying the feelings as right. For the moment, we're just feeling the emotion as directly as we can. There may be an accompanying storyline: "I like this feeling" or "When will it go away?" Despite this, we continue to lean toward the sensation itself, again and again.

Fear is intelligent, carrying a message about our situation, emotions, relationships, disconnections, and connections. My first Buddhist meditation teacher, the Venerable Chögyam Trungpa Rinpoche, called this "working with our negativity." He emphasized that some of what we often try to throw away as emotional garbage and entirely "negative" has a great deal to teach us about being alive and being human. When we practice this exercise, we become more comfortable with the experience of that emotion.

Find Your Home Ground
in a Stressful Moment

Sometimes in a stressful moment, like before a big presentation or when we are waiting for the results of recent medical tests, we may feel immobilized by our physical sensations and the stories our minds tell us. This is a perfect opportunity to let the mind be with the body—a familiar home ground, a safe foundation.

STEP ONE

Sit comfortably in your chair, self-supporting, with your back away from the back of the chair and your feet flat on the floor. Place your palms down on your thighs, and lower your chin slightly. If your eyes remain open, let your gaze fall toward the floor.

STEP TWO

Feel the bottoms of your feet on the floor. Feel the parts of your legs—the ankles, calves, and thighs. Feel your waist—and relax any excess tension there. Feel the torso, the lower back, the upper back, and the shoulders, relaxing these areas.

STEP THREE

Feel the back of your neck, the back of your head, the top of your head, and your forehead. Relax your eyes, cheeks, and jaws. Pay particular attention to unclenching your jaw. Relax. Feel the front of your body—stomach, waist, and flat bottom pressing on the chair.

STEP FOUR

Having felt the parts of the body, bring your attention to the whole body at once, the global body. Sit silently for a few minutes. During this time, if you find your attention wandering, gently return your attention to the seated body. Do this again and again, as needed. Stay with the bare sensation of the body as long as you can.

STEP FIVE

Return to a comfortable standing position, paying attention to your body's alignment—leaning neither forward nor back, not rigid, and not slumping. Treat the standing body as your familiar home ground. Let the mind be with the body for as long as you can.

If you can't take a seat, perform this body scan practice from a standing position, as described in step 5. For example, if you feel overwhelmed before delivering a speech, take a few moments to find your home ground.

The mind can start spinning out into storytelling mode during times of stress and anxiety, causing the body to react and prepare for fight or flight. This exercise can help break the cycle by shifting your attention back to your body, giving room for your thoughts to slow down. The mind-body connection is a two-way street, so encouraging your body to relax can help your mind relax, too.

six

Breaking Bad Habits or Negative Behaviors

Fresh! White

is a Certified Professional Co-Active Coach (CPCC), mindfulness teacher, writer, and facilitator. He supports executives, entrepreneurs, artists, and other coaches with achieving their goals and dreams.

Until about 15 years ago, I had a serious and long-time habit of going to bars and drinking several times a week. Once I changed those habits, I learned I had lingering negative behaviors, which for me were much harder to change. I found that I was argumentative, wanting to be "always right," and would catch myself preparing for my response while others were speaking. Beginning a new relationship and a new career, I knew I needed to change the way I was communicating to be successful. My mindfulness practice not only helped me see which behaviors I wanted to change, but it also helped me do so with patience and compassion for myself.

The Challenge

Living in a time when what used to take minutes now takes mere seconds, we may feel demands on us to be at the ready, if not ahead of everything. We might check our e-mail before we get out of bed in the morning, stay up late at night on social media to keep current, or cut people off in conversations to get our point across quicker, because we have trained ourselves to believe there is a benefit to these behaviors—such as "saving time" or "being productive."

Still, a part of us knows these behaviors are not serving us, and stopping them may seem impossible. In addition, our communities and environments actually encourage some of our negative behaviors, adding an extra layer of challenge.

Change is especially hard if we are not aware of the triggers or thoughts that precede the behavior. To change, it helps to know the reason for the behavior in the first place—the "cause and effect." Changing unwanted behaviors can be even harder if we have convinced ourselves that in practicing them there is some sort of reward—emotionally or physiologically. For example, I love people, but it wasn't until after I stopped drinking that I figured out I'm actually an introvert who feels a little shy around them. When sober, I prefer smaller groups and deeper conversations; I used drinking to help me get past my inhibitions and become the "life of the party." But this way of being and this type of communication didn't help me to connect in healthy ways.

How Mindfulness Helps

Being mindful requires us to be in the moment with whatever is happening within or around us. A regular mindfulness practice allows us an opportunity to be more present and aware, so that we can be more in choice when it comes to behaviors we want to change.

For example, within a week or so of when I first started practicing mindfulness regularly, I would notice my heart rate speeding up in the midst of certain conversations at work. For a while, I just ignored it. Then I started to investigate the emotions that arose when it was happening, and what I discovered was stress and fear. Soon I decided to pull back and quietly listen until my body calmed. By acting with more intention, I found myself more at ease when deciding whether or not to share my thoughts. Through listening and paying attention to my feelings, I learned a great deal about how different phrases or voice tenors caused reactions in my body, and just as important, I learned more about the people I was engaging with. The latter helped me see them more clearly and make fewer assumptions. With practice, I could shift to being at ease in conversations, and as a result, others seemed to reach out more often to share life or work experiences with me.

Many of our habits are so ingrained in our daily lives or systems. With a consistent mindfulness practice, you will witness yourself becoming aware of what you're feeling, which can allow you to pause just long enough to stop yourself from practicing a behavior that no longer serves you. The amount of time it takes for a mindfulness practice to show its benefits differs from person to person. It's important to be both consistent and patient.

What You Can Do

Setting yourself up to succeed at changing bad habits or negative behaviors requires a mindful attentiveness to yourself and your actions. Mindfulness can help you be present with and aware of what encourages you to behave in certain ways, so that you can better manage or change your habits, and reduce stress. Remember, in order to change, we have to do something different from what we usually do. Here are some tips to support you:

- *Set your intention.* When you make a conscious and formal commit-ment to something, you are telling yourself that *now is the time you are ready for change*, which will support your success. Here are a few ideas you may find useful:

  Write in a journal "why" you want to change; spell out how you will feel once the change has occurred. What will it free you up for? How will it make you different?

  Write your commitment on a sticky note using the present tense. For example, "I am glad to choose healthy food options to nourish my body today." You can post this in your bathroom, kitchen, or on mirrors as a reminder of your intention.

  Clear your space. For example, if you are quitting smoking, remove from your view anything associated with smoking, such as matches, ashtrays, and lighters.

- *Set reasonable and kind goals.* Choose to begin with one habit or behavior you want to change. Set a time limit. Change will take some patience; you will want to begin with no less than 30 days (90 being ideal), giving yourself room to begin again with kindness, should you backtrack. Remember, your mind thinks your habit is a natural behavior. Being kind during this transition allows you to experience the change as a good thing; you don't want to chastise yourself for any setbacks. Self-punishment may cause more fear that inadvertently encourages you to stop. Make failing a part of your process, and with patience and kindness, you will achieve your goal.

- **Work with an ally.** Share your goals and intentions with supportive confidants, personal or professional. You may ask them to support you with kind and patient check-ins to help you stay accountable. Having witnesses to our progress can be very supportive. If you do not have someone you trust, writing out and revisiting your commitments, as previously mentioned, can be really useful.

- **Practice mindfulness daily.** Mindfulness allows us an opportunity to be present. From here, we can better see and "choose" how we want to be in any moment. Through practice, we may begin to ask ourselves, "What am I *really* needing in this moment?" Perhaps we will notice that everything is great! Or perhaps we will realize that instead of needing our usual cigarette or snack, what we really want are some words of comfort or extra rest.

- **Don't give up!** It can take anywhere from 60 to 90 days to develop a new practice or break an old habit. It's common to experience resistance to any changes you may try to implement, especially if the old habit seems entrenched in your life and you feel like your sanity depends on it. Be patient. Mindfulness practices can very easily seem like a waste of time, one that's too difficult to fit into a busy schedule; it might seem like nothing is happening because it is so new and requires little action. If necessary, offer yourself a treat or a prize for the first 7 to 10 days for whenever you practice, or get an accountability partner to help strengthen your commitment. Some people even announce personal changes on social media to get support from their extended community. Whatever you do, stick with it. Know you can do it and that you're worth it!

Setting Daily Intentions

*I*ntentions allow us an opportunity to be more of who we want to be every day. For example, when you set an intention "to be especially kind to yourself," you may find yourself taking longer breaks, sitting down for a meal instead of eating on the run, or being more conscious of how you are treating yourself throughout the day. Keep things very simple, and remember, being committed is half the work. Use sticky notes, notifications on your phone, or other reminders to help you remember your intention. Let's say, for the sake of this exercise, that you set an intention to be more present with your breath throughout your day.

STEP ONE

When you wake up in the morning, set your intention: "I will practice being more present with my breath today."

STEP TWO

If you have a smartphone, set a reminder to go off every three hours to prompt you to be present with your breath. If you don't have a smartphone, use whatever tool you use to monitor and achieve your goals throughout the day. The idea is to find a way to add this exercise to your list of daily tasks.

STEP THREE

When your reminder prompts you, or you notice that it's time, begin by taking in one deep, slow breath through your nose. Then release it through slightly parted lips. This breath should be taken with ease. There is no need to force or exaggerate anything.

STEP FOUR

Take your second breath. As you release the breath, gently drop your shoulders. See if you can relax your arms and hands.

STEP FIVE

Take your last and third breath. See if you can hold your in-breath for a short moment before slowing and easily releasing your out-breath. Then begin breathing normally. Refresh with a drink of water, if available.

The more you practice, the more present you will be. Practicing once at the top of each hour or anytime you remember your intention will help you get better at noticing when the desire to perform a behavior that no longer serves you arises. From there, you'll be better able to choose how to respond.

If you are practicing a new skill around other people, you might think that they'll notice or ask questions. The great thing about this practice is that you are only taking deep, silent breaths; there's no need to exaggerate your breathing. Practice with gentleness and ease.

If three slow, mindful breaths feel like too much right now, consider taking a mindful sigh—feel the breath entering and filling your lungs, and then feel the release as you let your breath out. If you only have time to take one breath, go for it as often as you can! Everyone has time to breathe, right?

Mindful Self-Forgiveness

Knowingly or unknowingly, we may step over our intentions and repeat a behavior we already agree no longer serves us. Practicing self-forgiveness allows us to be patient with ourselves as we move into being more of the person we want to be. This exercise instructs you to reflect back on the day's events, but you don't have to wait until the end of the day. Self-forgiveness at any moment will help you experience the rest of your day with more ease and increase your awareness of your triggers.

STEP ONE

Sit comfortably, while also maintaining an erect, but not stiff, posture.

STEP TWO

Take three slow, deep breaths in and out, really taking your time. Then come back to normal breathing.

STEP THREE

Scan your day slowly, remembering, but not clinging to, moments when you may have harmed yourself or wished you had done something different.

STEP FOUR

As memories come up, simply say, "I have caused myself harm by _____, and I forgive myself." Then take a slow, deep breath. Do this for each incident that comes to mind.

STEP FIVE

Close the practice by taking three slow, deep breaths. With each inhalation, acknowledge any pain that may have arisen. With each exhalation, release that pain and thank yourself for being kind in this way.

Take your time with this practice; don't push yourself. When you are first starting out, take just a minute or two. As you feel more confident and comfortable, you may expand this to 5 minutes, and then 10 minutes or more. If you can acknowledge only one thing, no matter how trivial, it will be enough. You can increase weekly or monthly—whatever is most helpful for you.

Self-kindness practices may be difficult at first, especially when we are more used to being self-critical. Don't worry if you find this hard. There was a time I was so mad at my younger self that I would say flat out "no" to self-forgiveness. Other times, I seemed to forget or not have time for this practice. These are obstacles, and they may fade slowly. Remember, you are committed to making this change for the long term. Alone or with the help of a professional, you can choose to look at the obstacles that might be keeping you from doing this practice. But do so with gentleness.

Taking time in the middle of your day to see how you are doing may allow you another opportunity to offer yourself forgiveness. It needn't be formal. Take a moment while walking to or from lunch to review your morning, and see if there's something you want to forgive yourself for. This allows you to begin your afternoon with fewer burdens.

Morning Pages

Julia Cameron, author of *The Artist's Way* and other self-actualizing books, wrote, "The bedrock tool of a creative recovery is a daily practice called Morning Pages." Morning Pages is a stream-of-consciousness style of journaling ("free writing") that allows us to discover some of the patterns that may lead to our performing our unwanted behaviors. Purchase or find a new notebook and an easy-flowing pen for this project. Ideally, you'll want to create time and space to be able to write for up to 30 minutes over the next 30 days. If possible, do it the same time every day. However, even if you only have 5 or 10 minutes, doing this practice for 30 days will help you solidify this into a good habit that feels like a natural part of your daily experience.

STEP ONE

Set yourself up in a space where you can write for an uninterrupted period of time. Take three slow, deep breaths, exhaling slowly each time and dropping your shoulders; feel your feet on the floor.

STEP TWO

Place your pen on a clean page and set the intention of writing for the full amount of time allotted. Then begin writing whatever comes to your mind, and try not to stop. Even if all you can write is, "I don't want to write today," keep writing; something more will eventually come. Whatever you do, please don't judge or edit yourself. Be patient and kind—you are in a learning process.

STEP THREE

Once you've completed your time, pause and take a deep breath. See how you feel. Do you want to continue writing, review your writing, or move on with the rest of your day? It's your choice now that you've completed your commitment to write.

Many believe that our minds are the clearest in the morning when we first wake up, making it easier to connect to what's going on within us. However, writing in the morning won't work for everyone. So, although "morning" is included in the title of this practice, you can do this exercise whenever seems most convenient to you; in fact, I encourage this. To set yourself up to succeed, choose a time and place that is convenient and pleasant for you—at home, in a café, in the office during breaks, or outside.

When you find yourself hesitating or creating excuses not to write, follow the One-Minute Breath Meditation practice on page 30. When you are done, decide from there if the journaling practice is important at that time. Remind yourself that your commitment is your key to success.

This is free writing. If you are inspired to write for an hour or more, go for it. Just remember to be mindful of your body and don't let yourself burn out. If you find this exercise is too long to fit into a particularly busy day, take the notebook with you just in case you can capture a free moment in your schedule.

seven

Working with Attachments and Aversions

Acharya Fleet Maull

is a meditation teacher and social entrepreneur working to bring the healing and transformative power of mindfulness to a suffering world.

You've looked forward to a planned weekend away with your partner, only to be told the week prior that your partner has committed to a work assignment that will disrupt your plans. You feel sad and disappointed, or perhaps hurt and angry or even resentful and jealous of your partner's other interests and commitments. You dread the idea of spending another weekend doing your same old routine. If you're not careful, the situation can explode into angry words, drama, and more heartache. What can you do in this situation and others like it? In other words, how can you release your attachment to what you wanted or expected to happen and find acceptance for an idea you don't necessarily like?

The Challenge

It is quite natural to become attached to things going our way or play-
ing out according to our expectations. Unfortunately, the universe
rarely cooperates with our personal agendas. A colleague of mine calls
expectations "planned resentments." Even when things do appear to
be going our way, how long will it last? The one thing we know for sure
about life is that everything changes and nothing endures. Of course,
it's hard to imagine living free of expectations, free of likes and dislikes, or what the mindfulness traditions call *attachments* and *aversions*.

Have you noticed how much your moment-to-moment state of mind
and behaviors are driven by your attachment to comfort and pleasure
and your aversion to discomfort and pain? How often do you find yourself avoiding underlying discomfort, emotional issues, or even just
boredom by mindlessly consuming addictive snacks or junk food, grab-
bing a smoke, reaching for another drink, or surfing the Internet? How
much time do you spend strategizing how to avoid uncomfortable or
challenging social or professional situations? How dependent have we
all become on our air-conditioned homes, offices, and cars, to say nothing of our smartphones and other digital devices? How quickly do we
become upset when things are not going our way, when others appear
to be following their own agendas at the expense of ours?

Many of our preferences, our likes and dislikes, appear to be deeply
ingrained, almost *hard wired*. Nonetheless, being strongly attached to
certain things and averse to others, while seemingly natural and all but
unavoidable, is surely a prescription for suffering.

How Mindfulness Helps

Fortunately, the practice of mindfulness offers hope. Exploring our
attachments and aversions with mindfulness and self-compassion,
we may find the key to loosening their often painful grip on our state

of mind. Mindfully attending to our moment-to-moment experience allows us to feel and observe the impulsive urge to mindlessly reach for another potato chip, play another game on our phone, or click "purchase" in our online shopping cart. Mindfulness is the first step in developing the capacity and presence of mind to choose whether or not to go along with such urges.

Mindfulness also allows us to experience a kind of spaciousness of mind that allows us to observe and explore these habitual patterns of reactivity and their underlying feeling states without being completely caught or lost in them. Over time, the practice of mindfulness helps us access a more peaceful and equanimous way of being, a sense of being okay with ourselves and comfortable in our own skin, and less in the grip of attachment and aversion.

What You Can Do

While mindfulness can be brought to any human activity like walking, talking, and eating, the formal practice of mindfulness meditation is where we develop the capacity to be more mindful in the midst of our daily activities. During sessions of mindfulness meditation, we can closely observe our aversion to uncomfortable sensations in the body. We can also observe our attraction to pleasant experiences of peace and relaxation that may arise. With practice, we build a greater capacity to be self-reflective and develop more awareness of, and relaxation with, our moment-to-moment experiences of attraction and aversion.

The Don't Scratch the Itch . . . Not Just Yet practice on page 92 can be very helpful in cultivating this. This helpful exercise encompasses what seems like the simplest and hardest thing for a person to do—remaining very still even when an acute urge to scratch an itch arises. If we are willing to resist that impulse even briefly and examine the experience we are calling *itch*, we may be surprised to find that this seemingly solid and unpleasant experience is made up of a whole field of sensations, not all of which are unpleasant. We may notice that these underlying sensations are continually changing, here one moment, then gone, then somewhere else, and all pervaded by and surrounded by space. In some cases, we might even witness this collection of sensations completely dissolving; no more itch, discomfort gone!

Another approach is to work with the very root of our attachments and aversions—the fear and anxiety we experience due to never having fundamentally made peace with ourselves and the groundlessness of our experience. We lack a fundamental sense of home and continually look outside ourselves for a reason to feel good about ourselves or hopeful about our lives. Mindfulness itself is a means for coming home, actually occupying our physical, mental, and emotional bodies and making friends with our fears and anxieties. The more we come home, the more we begin to sense an unmistakable and innate wholeness, integrity, and goodness at the core of our being. We discover that we actually are okay . . . that we are not broken or missing anything, and that others are okay as well.

Finally, any time we are having a particularly good life experience, it is helpful to savor that, to really take it in and own it, so as to counteract our brain's tendency to focus on the negative, or what has been called the *negativity bias*. Current brain research tells us that we need to hold positive experiences in our attention, on the front stage of our brains so to speak, for 12 to 20 seconds for these experiences to go into long-term memory, whereas negative or fearful experiences go immediately into long-term memory. The Safe, Resourced, and Connected Contemplation practice on page 96 is very helpful for countering our negativity bias.

"

*A feeling of aversion
or attachment towards
something is your
clue that there's work
to be done.*

—Ram Dass,
Author and spiritual teacher

"

Don't Scratch the Itch . . .
Not Just Yet

Mindfully embracing and exploring uncomfortable or even painful sensations in the body allows us to notice the subtle way they're always changing, and helps us free our mind from the grip of aversion. As our attention stabilizes, we can notice the way in which we experience physical sensations as pleasant, neutral, or unpleasant. Given the challenges of sitting relatively still and erect, we will likely have a host of unpleasant sensations to choose from. We will likely experience strong aversion and the impulse to relieve the itch by scratching or the temptation to relieve pain by moving our body.

STEP ONE

Sit on a cushion or chair with a relaxed, uplifted posture. Allow yourself to feel and relax into the physical presence of your body.

STEP TWO

Notice your breath, paying attention to the physical sensations of breathing. Notice the air moving in and out of your nostrils, the rise and fall of your chest, and your weight on the seat. If thoughts arise, notice them without judgment and then return to your breath. Continue this practice until you feel relatively present and able to attend to your experience.

STEP THREE

Locate an uncomfortable or painful sensation in your body and gently place your attention there. Examine all the different sensations—is there a tingling, or numbness? Warmth, or cold?

STEP FOUR

Notice how the sensations come and go or change location. Notice that your mind is witnessing your body experience these sensations. Rest your mind in this awareness, this space between your physical experience and your mind's observation of it. Try to stay with this unpleasant sensation as long as you can.

STEP FIVE

When the aversion you feel is nearly overwhelming, repeat steps 2–4 once more, exploring a different unpleasant sensation this time.

STEP SIX

End the practice by taking three deep breaths, and thank yourself for taking the time to do this practice.

After learning this practice during meditation, you can easily do it anywhere—during a meal, standing in line, or lying in bed.

While exploring an unpleasant sensation, you might get lost in *mind chatter* about the unpleasant experience and a desire to react. Gently resist giving in by shifting your attention to something else, like neutral body sensations. If you meet your edge and give in to the impulse to move, do so without harsh judgment—you're only human. Then return to mindfulness of breathing practice until you feel present and able to attend to your experience with some degree of equanimity and curiosity.

Surfing the Urge:
Exploring the Mind of Craving

*C*ravings often arise and crest much like a wave. By learning to surf these waves of desire, we learn to be with the feelings of discomfort with greater ease and patience. With more practice, we learn that these cravings don't last; like all things, they eventually ebb away. We build our resilience so that we can eventually free ourselves from the often painful grip of attachment or even addiction.

STEP ONE

Sit quietly on a cushion or chair with a relaxed, uplifted posture. Allow yourself to simply feel and relax into the physical presence of your body.

STEP TWO

Begin to notice your breath, paying attention to the physical sensations that come with breathing.

STEP THREE

Continue the basic practice until you notice any kind of craving or desire arising in the mind or body. It could be a craving for food or a desire to move or do something different.

STEP FOUR

Rest your mind or awareness on the craving, just riding or *surfing* the energy or feeling of attachment. Let yourself feel it in your body and explore the different sensations that arise and fade away. Notice how the experience changes as you attend to it, embrace it, and ride its energy.

STEP FIVE

Notice that your mind is witnessing the part of you that is feeling craving or desire. Rest your mind in this awareness, this space between your craving mind and your observation of this craving mind. Try to stay with this as long as you can.

STEP SIX

When the craving you feel is nearly overwhelming, repeat steps 2–6 once more, exploring a different desire this time.

STEP SEVEN

End the practice by taking three deep breaths, and thank yourself for taking the time to do this practice.

It can be very helpful to do this practice on the spot if you catch yourself in a strong attachment or aversive reaction. Take a moment to check in with your craving. Simply stop and inquire within: "What am I feeling?" Remind yourself it's natural to feel cravings and take a few deep breaths, focusing on the body, so that you can give yourself a break from your mind chatter.

While attempting to explore a particular craving or desire, we may find ourselves giving in to that desire and acting on the urge. As with all mindfulness practices, gentleness, self-compassion, and humor are always important. We can simply return to the practice of mindfulness, acknowledge where we are, and begin again.

Safe, Resourced, and Connected Contemplation

Bringing the gentle and self-compassionate focus of mindfulness to attachments and aversions can be effective in lessening their often painful grip on the mind and sometimes troubling and limiting impact on behaviors. The following contemplation is adapted from the work of Rick Hanson, a neuropsychologist and author of *Buddha's Brain*. This practice has the potential to transform our negativity bias, encouraging a sense of well-being, positivity, and even happiness. Note: "Resourced" means having all of the resources required to function properly.

STEP ONE

At a time and place where you feel safe and resourced, sitting quietly with a relaxed, comfortable posture, allow yourself to simply feel and relax into the physical presence of your body. Notice your breath, paying attention to the physical sensations that come with breathing until you feel relatively present and able to focus your attention.

STEP TWO

While staying grounded in your body and breathing, contemplate the reality that right here, right now, *I'm safe*, bringing this to mind again and again as the experience of being safe. Contemplate the reality that right here right now, *I'm resourced . . . my basic needs are met*, bringing this to mind again and again as the experience of being resourced.

STEP THREE

Next, contemplate the reality that right here right now, *I'm connected . . . I have people in my life,* bringing this to mind again and again as the experience of being connected with other human beings.

STEP FOUR

Rest in the experience of feeling *safe, resourced,* and *connected,* mixing this with your mindfulness of breath.

It is possible, especially if you've had such experiences, that in contemplating the quality of feeling safe, memories or fears of feeling unsafe will surface. This is completely normal. Allow whatever arises to be there with compassionate acceptance and without judgment, while at the same time coming back to, "Yes, and nonetheless at this very moment I am safe." The approach is always one of gentleness, patience, and self-compassion.

Contemplating the qualities of feeling resourced and connected may bring up memories or fears about not being resourced or feeling alone or disconnected. Working with these experience with the same gentleness and compassion, we simply bring our mind back to, "Yes, and nonetheless at this very moment, I am resourced, I am connected to other human beings." It can be helpful to visualize our loved ones, close friends, and colleagues and really take in and own the fact that we *are* connected to others.

eight

Managing Anger and Hurt

Lama Rod Owens

is an authorized lama in the Kagyu school of Tibetan Buddhism. He is interested in the intersection of contemplative practice, identity, and social change.

One evening I was walking across a notoriously busy intersection on my way home when a car came speeding toward me. I assumed the gray sedan would eventually slow to a stop, obeying the stop sign and yielding to my right of way. It did not slow down. With my heart pounding, I sprinted out of the way. In shock, I looked back as the car screeched to a halt. The driver, a man my age, stuck his head out the window and wailed a howling, throaty jeer. He sped away without a care. I could have been killed, and I felt nothing but anger. I am not alone in experiencing a disruption that triggers a response of anger. That day, my mindfulness practice helped me look beneath my experience of anger into the hurt I felt, and care for it.

The Challenge

Anger is an expression of aggression that is triggered when we feel hurt or wounded. The aggression itself is our struggle to notice and accept the feelings of hurt. The hurt itself may stem from basic experiences of fear, injustice, offense, or physical pain. When these experiences of hurt arise, it can become difficult to simply notice the hurt without trying to distract ourselves from it. Anger is born when we believe we need to protect ourselves from the hurt, and thus we engage in a reaction that is often based on striking out at who or what has caused us harm.

It's hard to let go of anger because it is an experience that is so ingrained in our daily lives. Often we do not actually feel the anger because the experience can be very subtle; we may not be aware that we are angry. But this subtle experience can manifest as aggression in situations and interactions with a harmful outcome; it can cause us to lash out. When we do notice anger, it is difficult to recognize that beneath the anger is an experience of hurt that needs our attention. Moreover, many of us find that we are attached to anger because we feel that it is a motivator to get things done and to address the wrong that we have experienced.

Anger is worsened primarily in two ways. First, when we let narratives spin about how our anger is justified, our feeling of agitation is perpetuated. Second, when we respond to anger, we often act in a way that ends up being harmful or even violent. We see this each day often in the form the arguments, fights, or more tragically in the form of mass shootings and other acts of terrorism. It all stems from our basic struggle to notice and accept our feelings of being hurt.

How Mindfulness Helps

Mindfulness helps us diffuse the often-stifling experience of anger. Anger arises out of tightness and contraction in our mental experience that prevents us from noticing our underlying hurt. Mindfulness of the breath or body can shift our attention to a neutral experience that helps disrupt the automatic thought patterns or stories that frequently feed anger, and thus helps us see the hurt beneath anger. Mindfulness can help us recognize that anger is a signal that points to the presence of hurt in our experience. Anger is a wake-up call. When we know that anger is telling us that we are actually hurt, we are able to practice self-care to address our discomfort.

Mindfulness also helps us take responsibility for our anger. It is very easy to blame others for our anger. And though we may understand that others have hurt us, mindfulness helps us see that engaging in anger is a choice we make. When we take responsibility for our anger, we empower ourselves to work with it and take care of our hurt while blaming others less. Taking care of our hurt helps us find relief.

What You Can Do

To take care of our hurt, we must first give ourselves the space to notice our anger without staying in a position that can feed it. Often our anger is lessened when we take time to do something that makes us feel good. The experience of feeling good can also take our minds off of the disruptive emotion long enough to notice the hurt beneath it. Some feel-good activities include watching a favorite TV program, exercising, eating delicious food, resting, practicing yoga, talking with a trusted friend, and reading.

Practicing mindfulness techniques, both when we are feeling calm and when we are experiencing anger, helps us work with our anger to resolve the underlying pain. It can be difficult to remember to practice mindfulness when we are angry. That is a normal experience, especially when we are new to this practice. One way to increase our chances of remembering is to try the following practices during times when we feel calm, too. These practices can be done anywhere, but a quiet place where we can be alone with our thoughts and feelings for a few minutes is best.

Noticing How Anger Feels

To work with anger, we must learn how to notice the energy of anger even in its subtle expressions. This practice trains us to perform a quick inventory to recognize how anger feels in the moment, as well as additional emotions like sadness or fear that may arise with it. Having awareness of how our mind and body transition in and out of different emotional states can help us move away from angry states when they occur.

STEP ONE

Notice the presence of anger. Find a quiet place and sit comfortably. Think of a time when you felt a little bit angry. Pick an event that is not too intense, maybe a 4 or a 5 on a scale of 1 to 10, where 1 is mild irritation and 10 is overwhelming fury. Allow the memory to bring back some difficult thoughts and emotions.

STEP TWO

Practice curiosity. Ask yourself, "What am I feeling in this moment? In which part of my body am I feeling this? How does it feel?" Make a mental note of what you are feeling in any way that makes sense. For example, I will often notice my heart pounding and my blood rushing through my veins. The anger can feel uncontrollable or primal.

STEP THREE

Try to name sensations. Challenge yourself to name the physical and mental sensations you are experiencing to identify how anger uniquely functions in you. Make a mental list. My list may include narrowing in, no air, no room, and no choice.

STEP FOUR

Notice how anger feels good. We are often trained to identify uncomfortable aspects of anger; however, looking at how anger can feel pleasant can offer insight into how we form attachments to anger. Again, make a mental list, and above all be honest. My list includes insights like feelings of vitality, aliveness, jolting, directness, and power. Reflect on your list. Ask yourself how responding to these attachments have created harm for yourself or others. Try to make a commitment to notice your response to anger in the future.

This mindfulness practice may not be helpful in a situation when your anger is starting to rise in a quick, direct way. When that happens, walk away from the situation and refrain from interacting with others. Simply explain that you are upset and need to take a break because you do not want to do or say anything that could worsen the situation. Then engage in an activity that helps you feel more relaxed.

As you become more practiced at noticing how your body responds to anger, start paying attention to how your body responds to other emotions, such as sadness or fear. Noticing specifically how the body responds in different ways to different emotions is a tool we can use to identify how we are feeling, even if we cannot notice it in our minds. It may be helpful to keep a journal and record how your body responds as it moves in and out of certain emotional states.

Grounding Ourselves

Mindfulness of the body is an important strategy for helping us focus our attention away from anger. Bringing attention to our body through this grounding practice can help us feel a sensation of slowing down, even if our minds are racing ahead. Slowing down helps us feel more control over our responses to anger. Mindfulness of the body helps me ground my attention in a way that feels like a solid foundation.

STEP ONE

Notice the weight of your body. Bring your attention to your feet, feeling them firmly on the ground. Notice the weight of your body. If you are sitting, also notice the weight of your body on the seat. Ask yourself, "Can I trust the ground or the seat to hold me?"

STEP TWO

Relax. Relax into the ground and the seat. Imagine that whatever tension you feel in your body begins to dissolve and drain out through the ground under your feet and through the seat under your sitting bones.

STEP THREE

Notice what is around you. As you relax, begin to notice other sensations like sounds, scents, or perhaps colors. Just notice them for a few moments.

Sometimes it is difficult to let go of our thoughts. One helpful activity is performing a body scan, which invites you to place your attention on the different parts of your body. For a good body scan practice, see Find Your Home Ground in a Stressful Moment on page 72.

The connection between the body and the brain is a two-way street; during a stress response, the brain and the body influence each other. This is why the body gets tense when our mind is agitated, and why our body can relax when the mind is calm. This is also why grounding the body and encouraging your muscles to relax can be helpful in reducing the intensity of anger.

Contacting the Hurt
Beneath the Anger

When you are experiencing feelings of anger, try to be patient with yourself. When we practice patience, we are allowing our energy to move and shift, to loosen and clear up, which helps the anger thin out some. When the initial experience of anger softens, it is easier to see that anger has been guarding feelings of deep hurt. Shifting our attention to the hurt and realizing our need for love and compassion helps diminish the intensity of anger. The following steps can be taken wherever you might be.

STEP ONE

Notice other emotions besides anger. Try to notice the anger without responding to it or dwelling on the stories and thoughts that surround it. As you do so, turn your awareness to the other emotions that begin to arise. Often these emotions are ones of hurt. Allow yourself to turn toward that hurt instead of pushing it away, and look for physical sensations in the body. Where in the body do you feel these emotions?

STEP TWO

Relax into these difficult emotions. Notice how you react, physically and mentally, to uncomfortable emotions, while challenging yourself to relax and accept that these feelings are present, here in this moment. Try to relax your body and mind further even as you explore how these emotions feel in the body. Are they pleasant, neutral, or unpleasant?

STEP THREE

Remember that other people are feeling the same way you feel. Anger, hurt, sadness—these are all a normal part of being human. Other people experience similar kinds of hurt that have been guarded by anger. Reflect on the understanding that you are not alone in this experience.

If you feel overwhelmed by the hurt you uncover, give yourself permission to take a step back. It is okay not to focus on these feelings for a while or to just focus on bits of them at a time. Remember that you are not alone in these experiences; reaching out to others that you feel comfortable with can be helpful.

There is nothing wrong with feeling angry—emotions are okay. Exploring the physical component of anger in a gentle and nonjudgmental way can make it easier to let go of the thoughts and stories that feed anger. By identifying anger in the body, you help stop the fight or flight response that happens during stress.

Practicing Compassion

*C*ompassion is the wish to liberate ourselves and others from discomfort. The practice of compassion can teach us to accept what we are feeling and to understand that others are also suffering. Practicing compassion supports us in taking responsibility for our own discomfort even as it soothes our suffering. When we are able to do that, we can make a choice not to react out of anger. This practice can soften our animosity toward those we perceive have angered us and help us move deeper into the hurt under our anger.

STEP ONE

Receiving compassion. Place one hand over your heart; this is your center. Taking time to notice your hand there, repeat to yourself: "May I experience deep well-being, happiness, joy, and freedom from discomfort." Just keep repeating this to yourself and allow yourself to feel this wish for yourself.

STEP TWO

Sending compassion to others. Once you feel you are opening to this wish for yourself, you can chose to extend this wish to the person you are blaming for your anger. You can bring this person to mind and repeat: "May you experience deep well-being, happiness, joy, and freedom from discomfort." Just keep repeating this to yourself and allow yourself to feel this wish for the other person.

Initially, it may be difficult to send compassion to those who have hurt us. If we do not feel ready to send compassion to others, it can trigger resentment, which will feed back into our feelings of anger. Repeat step 1 over and over until you feel ready. Often, when we have worked with accepting compassion for ourselves long enough, we will feel a natural opening to send compassion to others.

Consider keeping a "prescription list" of self-care activities to choose from for those times when you are too upset to think clearly. These activities can be as simple as taking a five-minute walk or something more involved, like going to yoga class or getting a massage.

nine

Supporting Others Who Need Help

Maia Duerr

*is a writer, anthropologist, and ordained chaplain. She
believes in the power of contemplative practices to cultivate
compassion, awareness, and social transformation.*

For the third time this week, your phone rings at
11:30 p.m. and it's your sister. She's clearly had one
drink too many and she's crying as she recounts to you
the challenges of her week. She's lost her job (again)
and asks if you can help her with some money so she
can get groceries. You love your sister and want to
support her but wonder if that's the best way. It's easier
to not answer the phone and avoid the whole thing.
Still, your conscience nags at you. How can you help?

The Challenge

In our increasingly interconnected world, we constantly encounter people who need all kinds of help. They may be friends, coworkers, or our own family members. They may also be strangers in our neighborhood who need assistance, or people living across the globe who have experienced a terrible flood or other natural disaster.

We might become a caregiver for an aging parent. Perhaps a cousin needs one-time material assistance, like a loan to get him through until the next paycheck. Or maybe a friend asks for our emotional support and a shoulder to cry on. Sometimes the problems are so complex that we have no idea what the other person needs, and they may not be able to tell us.

We want to help, that much we know. We can feel the tug at our heartstrings. But we may be confused about how much support to offer and what's the "right" way to offer it. When does help do more harm than good? And how can we help if we are feeling lost in our own despair or anger, or we simply don't have the time or energy?

How Mindfulness Helps

A growing body of neuroscientific research indicates that compassion is a naturally occurring trait. But the circumstances of our busy lives and lack of training in how to cultivate compassion can make it difficult for us to access it. Mindfulness helps us reconnect with this inner resource so that we may offer it to others who need assistance. Through mindfulness, we can also develop self-compassion so that we don't crash and burn from our attempts to help another.

Mindfulness allows us to better regulate our own emotions when we are in a helping interaction, which in turn supports the other person. If they are overcome with anxiety or fear, our own calm response can assist them to find a place of equanimity and access their own coping skills.

When our efforts to help another are based in mindful awareness, we are more likely to give skillful support that makes a positive impact on the other person—and on us.

What You Can Do

Self-care and self-compassion, both attributes of mindfulness, are good starting points for a positive and sustainable helping interaction. Make sure to schedule regular breaks to take part in activities that nourish you, such as physical exercise, time with friends, listening to soothing music, or cooking a healthy meal. This is particularly important if you are acting as a long-term caregiver. No matter what kind of helping situation you are in, the Self-Compassion Break practice on page 116 will support you to take care of your emotional and spiritual needs.

One of the keys to offering effective help is understanding the difference between empathy and compassion. Empathy is our capacity to understand how another person feels, whether that's a pleasant feeling such as happiness or a challenging one such as pain or grief. Neuroscientist Tania Singer notes that empathy is a precursor to compassion, and that too much empathy can be problematic. If you find yourself overidentifying with another's situation and actually taking on their emotions, you may be stuck in empathy mode. This can lead to empathic distress and eventually burnout.

In contrast, when you feel compassion for another's suffering, you have a sense of what they may be feeling and you care about their pain, but you recognize that it is not your pain. This ability to differentiate allows you to feel warmth toward them and act in compassionate ways without becoming overwhelmed by their situation.

Empathy can be transformed into compassion through mindfulness practice. The G.R.A.C.E.® practice on page 120 is especially useful in this regard. Another simple way to begin the shift is to pay attention to what you are experiencing as you interact with the person you are helping. Then quietly label it as one of three sensations: pleasant, unpleasant, or neutral. This could apply to a physical sensation you notice (stress in your shoulders), an emotional one (joy at being of service to another), or a mental one (confusion). By increasing awareness of your own internal experience in a nonjudgmental way, you start a process of healthy differentiation that allows you to be more fully present to the other person.

Helping someone can be one of the most positive experiences of life, leading to gratitude, joy, and inspiration. We can actually feel better about ourselves when we support another. The following three practices invite you to harness the power of mindfulness and apply it to a helping interaction so that it has the best chance of becoming a rewarding experience for everyone involved. Without a base of mindful awareness, the helping interaction has the potential to evoke irritation, resentment, and other negative emotions.

> *If your compassion does not include yourself, it is incomplete.*

—Jack Kornfield,
Author and Buddhist teacher

Self-Compassion Break

This practice, based on the work of Dr. Kristin Neff, develops self-compassion in order to prevent burnout. Use this practice whenever you feel stressed, upset, angry, or other emotions that signal suffering. Or, think of a situation that is challenging for you, one that is bringing up physical and/or emotional suffering. As you call this situation to mind, notice any feelings of stress and emotional discomfort in your body. Then say the following three phrases to yourself:

STEP ONE

"This is a moment of suffering." Acknowledging what is true in this moment, without judgment, is the basic practice of mindfulness.

STEP TWO

"Suffering is a part of life." With this phrase, you recognize your connection to every other human being. Other phrases you can say include "Other people feel this way," "I'm not alone," or "We all struggle in our lives." As you say these words, place your hands on your heart, cheek, or belly and feel the compassion you are directing toward yourself.

STEP THREE

"May I be kind to myself." Offer yourself this sincere wish for
your own peace of mind. You may wish to add one or more of
these phrases:

*"May I give myself the
compassion that I need."*

*"May I learn to accept
myself as I am."*

"May I forgive myself."

"May I be patient."

You can use this practice as a way of taking care of yourself any
time you notice yourself feeling stress while helping another.

---

*At first it may feel difficult to send these wishes of loving-kindness
toward yourself.* If that's the case, begin by bringing to mind another
person whom you love dearly or even a beloved pet. Use these same
phrases with that person or animal in mind. Then, while the compassion is flowing, slip yourself into the stream by directing the phrases
toward yourself.

*If you are short on time, just focus on the third phrase, "May I be
kind to myself."* If you have extra time or want to go deeper into this
practice, you may enjoy reading *The Kindness Handbook: A Practical
Companion* by Sharon Salzberg and trying the "Loving-kindness"
practice that she includes.

Caring with Intention

*I*t's easy to go on autopilot when we offer help or care to another. When this happens, we can lose sight of the impact of our help on the other person. We may also neglect to take care of ourselves. As we become more intentional and aware of what we are doing and how we are doing it, we can use the power of mindfulness to make better decisions about how to offer help. The Caring with Intention practice can help turn too much empathy into compassion.

STEP ONE

If you begin to feel off balance in a helping interaction, take that as a sign that it's time to step back and get some perspective. Schedule a 15-minute block of time in your calendar for this "intention check." Do it as often as you need.

STEP TWO

During this "intention check" time, ask yourself the following questions and write down your responses:

- How are my actions actually serving the person I am trying to help? Are there any negative consequences to the kind of help I am offering them?

- Am I doing too much?

- What kinds of physical and emotional responses am I experiencing as a consequence of this helping relationship? Am I taking care of myself?

- If I feel overwhelmed by the tasks involved with taking care of another, can I ask for help for myself so that I don't have to do it all alone?

STEP THREE

Consider the answers to your questions and see what insights arise. Are there adjustments you may want to make so that this helping relationship feels more sustainable to you?

This practice is especially useful for long-term caregivers. If you are in this situation, make time at least once a month to reflect on these questions.

The biggest difficulty that might come up for you with this practice is actually remembering to do it! Schedule a date and time or ask a friend to keep you accountable to your commitment to self-care. Have them remind you these questions are important to review regularly. If you feel comfortable doing so, you can even share your answers with them and invite them to help you reflect on your situation.

G.R.A.C.E.®

Originally developed by Dr. Joan Halifax for clinicians working in end-of-life care, G.R.A.C.E.® has been used by therapists, social workers, chaplains, and others to assist in developing compassion as they interact with patients or clients. This simple and efficient practice can be used in any situation in which you are helping another. This is a practice you can use while in the presence of another person, but one that you do internally; the person you are helping does not need to know that you are moving through these steps.

STEP ONE

G—*Gather your attention.* Pause, take an in-breath, and give yourself time to get grounded. Focus your attention on your breathing or on a neutral part of your body where you feel no pain or discomfort, such as your hands.

STEP TWO

R—*Recall your intention.* Remember why you have chosen to help this person. Your motivation will keep you connected to the other person as well as to your own values.

STEP THREE

A—*Attune by checking in with yourself, and then the other person.* Notice what's going on in your own mind, body, and feelings. Then, without judgment, try to sense the experience of the other person. What emotional cues do you pick up?

STEP FOUR

C—*Consider what is going on in the present moment.* Notice insights that arise. What is the other person offering? What might best serve the person and the situation? Draw on your knowledge and experience; at the same time, stay open to seeing things in a fresh way.

STEP FIVE

E—*Engage with the person and end the encounter.* Compassionate action will emerge from the sense of openness, connectedness, and discernment you have created in the first four steps of this practice. Then recognize internally when the encounter is over by paying attention to your out-breath.

Like any practice, the more you use G.R.A.C.E.®, the more natural it becomes. Even if all you can do is remember step 1 (the "G" step) for one in-and-out-breath, it will make a difference in your capacity to be present to yourself as well as for others.

G.R.A.C.E.® is taught as part of a comprehensive training program offered at Upaya Institute and Zen Center in Santa Fe, New Mexico. If you are interested in learning more about this model, and how to use G.R.A.C.E.® in diverse situations, visit the website of the Upaya Institute (see Resources on page 149).

ten

Accepting Aging and Illness

Shahara Godfrey

is a graduate of the UCLA Mindful Awareness Research Center program and a core teacher at the East Bay Meditation Center. She is also a cancer survivor.

————————————

We all experience illness in our lives, which can feel disempowering and difficult at times. Meditation, yoga, and other exercises can help us be more aware as we work with health challenges. I recently faced a cancer diagnosis with intense treatment and complications. Mindfulness practice helped me get through it. While facing illness and aging are a normal part of the human experience, mindfulness practices can help us stay present with our suffering, consider our options, and find renewed joy and appreciation for life, regardless of the conditions we find ourselves in.

The Challenge

Aging and illness are part of the human condition because our bodies are constantly changing over time. We experience illness at different ages, as our body seeks to heal and rebalance itself. As we age, we may find our metabolism slows down, we are diagnosed with a new illness, or we take longer to recover from injury. We may also find we simply don't have the same energy or memory we did when we were younger. A 20-year-old body is very different from a 60-year-old one. Fatigue, chronic illness, diminished strength, body changes, and limited movement all can contribute in the inevitable process of aging.

How Mindfulness Helps

Many hospitals now incorporate Mindfulness-Based Stress Reduction (MBSR) into their services, which has helped many patients cope more effectively with stress, pain, illness, and aging. Mindfulness helped me through the early stages of healing from cancer and its aftermath; it continues to do so today. Before my cancer diagnosis, I thought such an illness would never happen to me. After diagnosis, I thought, *"This is my life. It's not what I expected, but how do I want to live it now?"* Along the way, even during times of intense pain, I realized that while nothing stays the same, and things do not always go as expected, I can be with what is right now. I had no way to predict what this cancer journey would be like, as I had not experienced it before. Though at times the conditions have been very difficult, mindfulness practice and staying present throughout the healing process have made a difference for me. By accepting these truths, I have learned to let go of attachments that can cause suffering (such as the wish for an unchanging, healthy body) and to stop pushing away aversions that are impossible to avoid (such as physical pain).

The following mindfulness practices have helped me navigate my health challenges with compassion and gentleness. My hope is they help you find some comfort and ease on your journey, too.

What You Can Do

While the experience of aging and illness is universal, it can also be a cause of great suffering. The challenge we have as humans is practicing acceptance of aging and illness as part of our journey, so we can encourage health and wellness at different parts of our life span.

At senior centers and hospitals across the country, programs exist to support elders and those with chronic illness or disability. For example, yoga and meditation training can be adapted for shorter periods while sitting in a chair instead of on the floor. If we don't have the time or resources to take classes, or if they're offered at locations that are inaccessible to us, we can seek out activities closer to home. A brief, mindful walk each day can be beneficial, whether we are able to move on our own, or need the assistance of a companion, cane, or walker. We can also connect with our family members and friends for support when we are ill, or join a support group for people struggling with chronic illnesses to exchange ideas about what can help us ease our pain and symptoms.

You can start practicing mindfulness with as little as a few minutes a day. The following exercises can help you become more aware of your body and its current conditions, or to cope with anxiety about a recent diagnosis. These exercises may also be useful for those who are caretakers for us or other family members as we age.

Mindfulness practices for illness and aging can help us be active participants and monitors of our health, and to focus on what we can do to improve our physical, mental, and emotional well-being. Mindfulness can also help us find acceptance about the conditions we cannot change, and it can cultivate the clarity we need to sit with our options for treatments without having to rush to a decision. Try these exercises throughout your day, and notice how you feel after practicing them for a while.

Be with What Is, Just in This Moment

*H*ave you ever wanted to change a situation or want it to be different than it is? Affirmations on acceptance can help us face the conditions we are in. Try doing this practice without any expectations, being with what is "just in this moment." This can be a powerful exercise in self-care.

STEP ONE

Find a comfortable place where you can sit and not be distracted. Turn off any media devices so you are not interrupted.

STEP TWO

Take a full breath, allowing yourself to slow down, then speak aloud this affirmation: "Be with what is, just in this moment."

STEP THREE

Pause briefly, and then take another deep breath. Then speak aloud the same affirmation again. Repeat two more times.

STEP FOUR

Sit quietly for another minute. Notice what you are thinking, feeling, and any bodily sensations you are experiencing. Close the practice with a final deep breath.

Mindfulness exercises can be practiced in small amounts of time, in different physical conditions, and from wherever you are. This practice can be done anytime you want a situation to be different, such as when you are waiting to get lab results or preparing to discuss treatment options. Affirmations can help rewire our thinking. These eight little words made a huge difference by helping me get through a challenging time during my cancer diagnosis and treatment.

Obstacles can arise when we are afraid and in instances where the outcome is unknown. You may feel resistance, anxiety, or not feel authentic when saying the affirmation. A large part of this exercise is to relax into the moment and to say it even though we may not feel it just yet. With repetition, our feelings might change in the future.

If you have additional time, you can experiment with the affirmation. You can chant it, sing it, speak it softly or loudly, or write it out on paper and decorate it as an art project. Once the exercise is completed, the situation may be unchanged, but you are not. Repeating this affirmation over time will shift your experience.

Gratitude for Life

When we think about aging and illness, sometimes we can forget what is important. A daily practice of gratitude for our life can help us feel differently about our health situation, perhaps even bringing us peace and joy.

STEP ONE

Find a quiet place where you can sit uninterrupted. Take out paper or a journal and something to write with. Then take three deep breaths.

STEP TWO

Ask yourself, "What parts of my body and health am I grateful for?" Write down five items. Be as spontaneous as possible.

STEP THREE

Review what you wrote. After each item, take a moment to reflect and notice any thoughts, feelings, or bodily sensations that arise. This could be a smile, laughter, or a reminder that some parts of your body are healthy at this moment.

STEP FOUR

Take a final deep breath and say thank you to your body for being alive.

This exercise can take place at home or in your workplace during a short break. You can also practice gratitude for your life and body as you are waiting to see your doctor.

This exercise on appreciating our health, our body, and our life can shift our perspective, especially about matters that are out of our control with regard to aging and illness. It may also give us the positive energy to focus on what we can do to improve our health. What parts of your body and health are you grateful for?

If you feel challenged to come up with your list, focus on one part of your body or health and what it allows you to do. The goal is to appreciate what may be overlooked or taken for granted. You can also try writing just one item per day or per week, until you arrive at five items.

If you have additional time, you can try doing this exercise with a family member or friend during a visit. You can also share it with a child you know to help spark your creativity and to teach them gratitude for life. You can also increase the number of items you are grateful for. Warning: this practice may become habit forming!

Taking a Pause

Taking a pause is a more common phenomenon than most people may know or realize. We do it all the time. Taking a pause helps us notice when mental commentaries or stories about our aging and health conditions run through our minds. A pause can also help us resist the pressure to make a rushed health decision, before we have had a chance to sort things out. Resting in the now helps us reflect on how we're doing, given our current health conditions. The goal is to not to do anything; we simply notice what is going on in our mind, our body, and our heart.

STEP ONE

Take a pause in the day. You may engage in this activity standing, lying down, or sitting. Find what is comfortable for you.

STEP TWO

Be in the present with intention and a deliberate focus on this very moment, right now. Breathe deeply, paying attention as your breath goes in and out of your body. Notice what is arising in the moment for you.

STEP THREE

After a minute or two has passed, expand your attention to places you feel discomfort or pain, or a part of your body that is experiencing illness, without the need to do anything about it.

STEP FOUR

Two minutes later, or when you are ready, take a final deep breath to close the exercise and go about the day.

This exercise can be done in the comfort of your own home, on your way to work, or at a comfortable location outside. You can also engage this practice when you are feeling frustrated or sad about your experiences of aging or illness, or while making a nourishing meal that will help your condition. Taking a pause can happen anywhere and anytime, without anyone knowing what you are doing! The opportunities for taking a mindfulness pause are endless.

One potential obstacle is the tendency to fall asleep, especially when we are experiencing chronic illness or fatigue. Try experimenting at different times of the day. You might find that your energy, pain, or discomfort vary throughout the day. Another obstacle can be the pain from staying in one position for too long. Feel free to adjust, stretch, or move as needed while continuing to focus on your breathing and the sensations in your body. If you have more time, consider doing it more than once a day or journaling about your experience.

You might have expectations around a specific outcome, or wonder if you are doing the exercise "right." Remember not to judge yourself for your thoughts, and try not to rush the experience. When your mind wanders, return to your breath. There is no right or wrong way of doing this, and noticing your hectic thoughts or distractions is just one more opportunity to return to your awareness right now, again and again. Remember, the situations and experiences you face are a normal part of life and do not define who you are. You are only human, and you're doing the best that you can. And if things feel overwhelming, have faith in the knowledge that whatever you're experiencing shall pass.

eleven

Coping with Grief and Loss

Kate Johnson

is a teacher, writer, and dancer who works at the intersections of meditation, art, and activism. She lives in Brooklyn, New York.

———

Loss can be disorienting. Whether we are grieving the loss of someone who was very close to us, or if we find ourselves, due to violence or disaster, grieving the losses of people we did not even know, facing the reality of death can make us feel as if our very foundations are cracking and slipping away. Other losses can lead to grief. The loss of a job, a relationship, a home, or other foundational parts of our lives can all be experienced with mourning. In this chapter, we approach mindfulness practice as a method for navigating grief, while building clarity, comfort, and capacity in the process. In a world that is uncertain and often unjust, we can start to find solid ground by allowing awareness to be our inner compass, helping us steady ourselves in the present moment, connect authentically with others, and eventually, to heal and grow.

Loss Hurts

Sometimes, the pain of loss comes on immediately sharp in its intensity. Other times, feelings of loss can spread slowly, like thick oil coating the surface of water. We can cycle through states of paralyzing fear, openhearted acceptance, breathtaking sadness, and hot rage within a span of hours, and then we can go totally numb for a time. There may be periods of feeling relatively normal, and then suddenly, we can find ourselves becoming overwhelmed once again.

All this is to say: the grief process is complex, varied, and personal. How grief shows up for us is dependent on so many factors. Our relationship with the person, people or things we have lost, the circumstances of those losses, the strength of our support networks, and our personal and cultural attitudes toward death, dying, endings, and change—are just a few of the conditions that can influence our grief experience.

Whatever the source or shape of your grief, if you are reading this chapter, you have likely discovered that trying to squash or shove the feelings of grief aside doesn't really work, and doesn't really make you any feel better. You're willing to explore ways of consciously working with your grief, and at least some part of you believes in your strength and capacity to bear this process consciously. This is good, this is better than good, because as much as loss hurts, the process of grief is one that can be healing. Grief provides us an opportunity to pause, to reflect on the realities of our relationships, to feel the preciousness of our own tender human life, and to choose to live fully, vividly, and lovingly.

Mindfulness Helps

Mindfulness is sometimes described as the felt sense that the mind, heart, and body are all connected and in harmonious relationship with one another. Strong grief pops us out of alignment, and can leave us feeling as if parts of ourselves are scattered and out of sync. When we are lost in obsessive thoughts or powerful emotions, or disconnected from our bodies, the nonjudgmental awareness of what is actually happening within us and around us can help bring us back to our senses. Mindfulness gets us in touch with our simple moment-to-moment sensory experience—feet on the floor, seat on the chair, contact of the hands, the chest expanding and softening with each breath—things that can help steady a racing mind or a heavy heart. Once we feel settled and secure, engaging the quality of mindfulness can help us feel as if we have a loyal friend sitting calmly by our side, witnessing us as we bring awareness to the thoughts and emotions that challenge us. When we can clearly see the reality of our inner landscape and our external circumstances, we gain the opportunity to choose how we will care for ourselves and others, rather than reacting out of habit in ways that may not serve us.

What You Can Do

If we could control our feelings, we probably would. The reality is— states of grief come and go on their own, without any invitation or permission from us. The best we can do, since grief comes anyway, is to choose ways to acknowledge and hold our grief gently, rather than struggling against it. This is akin to a willingness to uncover and clean a wound, airing it out in order to heal, instead of piling more bandages on top. Of course, we should take breaks when we feel flooded, and return to the present situation again when we feel capable of meeting it. The mindful approach is gradual, and incredibly simple, and we may feel like nothing at all is happening. But over time, we will build a powerful patience and endurance that will serve us, as well as our loved ones and our communities, in times of grief. And one day, we may look for our familiar grief and realize it has softened around the edges.

- *Know grief as grief.* Responses to loss can present in so many different thought patterns, emotional tones, and physical sensations. Feeling through these is all part of the healing process. The ups and downs of the landscape of grief aren't at all a problem unless we forget that they are in fact functions of our response to loss, and we take them to be the truth of who we really are. When the anger, sadness, impulsivity, or irritations arise, recognizing, "Ah, this is grief" can give us the gift of perspective. Knowing that these are temporary states of heart and mind, and reflecting on the ways in which they change, even over the course of a day, we are able to take them a little less seriously. Silently saying, "Ah, this is grief," we can remember that we deserve our own gentleness at this time, and we can choose to give ourselves and others a break, and find a way to express our grief that is nurturing and supportive.

- *Know the absence of grief.* One thing that surprises me about states of grief is that they are never constant. My idea about grief, before actually experiencing a profound loss myself, was that it would be like a wall, solid and relentless. My actual experience of deep grief when it finally happened to me was more like waves. Between peaks of heartbreak and mourning, there were moments of relative calm, ease, normalcy, and even joy. Grief subsides eventually, even if just for a few moments, and when it does it is helpful to notice, "Ah, grief is not here right now." Bringing mindful awareness to these gaps helps us consciously remember that this too shall pass. Knowing in these moments, "Ah, this is the absence of grief," we are not betraying the ones we have lost, and we are not in denial—we are in full presence of the reality of our own resilience.

- *Give it time.* Grief takes the time that it takes, and how much time that will be can't be known with any certainty. Don't abandon yourself if your grief process is taking longer than you think it should. One skillful practice is to create dedicated times throughout the day to care for your heart and honor that which was lost. I hope some of the following practices will help you structure grieving time in a way that is helpful and healing for you.

When pain is met with caring presence, something magical happens. The pain eases. It opens and unfolds like a bud in spring.

— Oren Jay Sofer,
Mindfulness and meditation teacher

Making Space in the Heart

*P*aying attention to the sensations of breathing in the chest can steady our minds and encourage a relaxing of the heart, accepting and making plenty of space for whatever is true for us in this moment.

STEP ONE

Set a timer for five minutes.

STEP TWO

Sit or lie down in a way that is comfortable, and allow your body and mind to be both alert and relaxed.

STEP THREE

Bring your attention to your heart space, in the center of your chest. Notice any sensations that are present there. Does it feel tight or spacious? Is it tender? Strong? Solid? Quivering? Observe the physical sensations with an attitude of caring awareness, not demanding that the heart feel any other way that it does. Offer your heart your loyalty by demonstrating the constancy of your awareness.

STEP FOUR

Notice the sensations of your breath right now. As you breathe in, breathe in deeply, allowing the space around your heart to expand fully. As you breathe out, soften the heart space, relaxing any tension around it. Continue to notice the breath sensations as they change, imagining that your breath is ventilating the space of the heart.

STEP FIVE

If you notice yourself getting lost in worries or judgments, gently bring your awareness back to your breathing.

STEP SIX

When the timer rings, take a moment to place your hand on your heart and acknowledge your bravery and kindness at the willingness to make more space for your experience of your heart, whatever it may have been.

If you find that focusing on the heart or the breath is agitating, you can practice being mindful of the sensations in the hands or the feet instead.

It is possible to work with this practice for just a few breaths at a time at almost any time—standing in line, sitting at your desk at work, or even in conversation.

Mindful Altar Ritual

Establishing a personal ritual, this time around an altar, makes space and time for the heavy heart to soften, surrender, and reconnect. This can eventually create a healthy boundary around remembrance to distinguish times of intentional mourning from the rest of daily life.

STEP ONE

Finding the right place. The best place for your altar is somewhere that is accessible and available. It doesn't have to be fancy—a windowsill, a corner of your desk, even the dashboard of a car.

STEP TWO

Setting up the space. Gather objects that are meaningful representations of your loss. These can be photographs, pieces of writing, drawn images, articles of clothing . . . anything that helps bring up the felt sense of who or what you want to remember and honor. One or a few objects will do. Place your items in the location you have designated.

STEP THREE

Making offerings. Take time to contemplate what you would like to give today. Flowers? Arrange them with care and place them in the altar space, holding in mind what they represent. A letter you wrote? Read it out loud and then place it in front of the altar. Food, stones, feathers, physical gestures—feel free to get creative in offering representations of the care and healing you wish to convey.

STEP FOUR

Being present. This is a quality that can be integrated throughout the mindful altar practice. Notice what sensations are present in your body as you consider, gather, and prepare your offerings. What thoughts and emotions come up, and what is your relationship to them? See if you can maintain a generally accepting awareness toward whatever sensations, feelings, or thoughts arise—they are all part of the unfolding of the grief process. Notice, too, if anything surprises you.

STEP FIVE

Closing the space. Find a way to end the ritual period and reenter the space of your daily life. Blow out the candles. Bow, wave, or verbally say goodbye, and then move into your next daily activity.

Decide how long you want your ritual period to last. Perhaps this is a one-time, one-day mourning period. Or another period of time that feels meaningful to you. At the end of that time, it's fine to dismantle the altar and redistribute the gathered items, or dispose of or donate them as feels appropriate. The love and energy you offered remains with you and in the space even after the ritual period ends.

Sometimes when preparing or performing rituals, doubt arises in the form of thoughts like, "This is silly." Notice these thoughts with mindfulness, thank them for their input, and then try the practice anyway, with an attitude of curiosity and a sense of openness.

Mindful Movement

Grief is an embodied experience, but when you are overwhelmed, it can make you feel numb or separate from your body. This practice helps reestablish presence in the body, and space to notice, care about, and follow sensation, letting the body's wisdom take the lead without judging it or controlling it (adapted from Acharya Arawana Hayashi's practice, "20 Minute Dance.")

STEP ONE

Set a timer for five minutes.

STEP TWO

Clear a space on the floor or bed where you can lie down and rest. Close your eyes—they can remain closed or just slightly, softly open for the rest of the practice.

STEP THREE

Notice sensations in the body. Where is there heaviness, or lightness? Warmth, or coolness? Tingling? Pulsation? Notice the feeling of the shape your body is making on the floor. Feel your body breathing.

STEP FOUR

While in this still shape, pay attention to when and where your body wants to move. It may be a part of your body or may be the whole body that wants to shift. Follow the feeling of "wanting to move" in whatever direction it takes you. Stay true to whatever your body feels like doing; give yourself permission to do that as long as you want.

STEP FIVE

Eventually, your body will want to return to stillness in some shape, either lying on the floor in some way, or sitting, or standing. Pause in that shape, allowing yourself to let go of whatever came before and rest in the sensations of the body and the breath until the next time your body wants to move again.

STEP SIX

Alternate moving and stillness until the bell rings to close the practice, paying equal attention to both aspects of the embodied experience.

Try this practice any time there is a lot of restlessness or heaviness your body, or when you feel stuck or numb. You can do this practice sitting at your desk, too. If time permits, feel free to try the practice for up to 20 minutes, giving yourself permission to move or rest during that time.

Often, thoughts or judgments might influence what your movement will look like or how you are or are not supposed to move. Or you will fall into habitual, tried-and-true movements rather than discovering in the moment a fresh movement your body wants now. Don't worry—just keep practicing and the habits will soften over time.

If there isn't time for a full mindful movement practice, bring awareness to sensations of your body as you go about daily activities—the texture of your food, the temperature of the water as you wash your hands—all of these can help bring you into your body and into the lived experience of this precious moment.

Acknowledgments

First, I wish to honor my family, parents Esmeralda and Carlos Salgado and siblings Debbie and Carlos, for modeling loving-kindness and generosity throughout my life. I also honor my beloved husband Rick Mannshardt for encouraging me on my path and being such a wonderful partner in life.

Second, I want to express my gratitude to my editor Clara Song Lee for the warm invitation to work on this book and her encouragement and support as I embarked on my journey as a new author. Her mindfulness, vision, patience, and guidance were such a gift on this project, and I am indebted to her for this opportunity. I am also deeply grateful to the skillful staff at Callisto Media for the many gifts they shared as they brought this book into fruition.

Lastly, I want to thank each and every one of the chapter contributors for their many years of dedication in bringing the teachings of mindfulness to so many people, across so many wide walks of life. You have collectively contributed so much to the healing and liberation in our world, and I am grateful for you.

Ten Tips to Deepen Your Practice

Perhaps after reading this book, you are curious about how you might deepen your mindfulness practice. Here are some tips to help you.

1. *Create a daily ritual that promotes mindfulness.* It can be a morning ritual, like doing a few stretches before you get out of bed, pausing to look out the window before pouring your coffee, and then savoring three sips of the coffee before going about your day. Pick a ritual that is enjoyable so you'll be more likely to stick with it.

2. *Commit to a daily mindfulness practice.* The practice does not have to be long; it can be as simple as checking in with your body for a few breaths. You can use an alarm or smartphone app like Insight Timer (insighttimer.com) to set daily reminders that keep you on track. Alternatively, you can choose an activity you do every day, such as brushing your teeth, and make that your regular mindfulness practice.

3. *Practice yoga regularly.* Because there is so much emphasis on paying attention to the breath and the body, practicing yoga is great for cultivating mindfulness. I recommend Seane Corn (seanecorn.com) and Hala Khouri (halakhouri.com) as great teachers for in-person training, retreats, and online courses. You can also browse online yoga classes at Do Yoga With Me (doyogawithme.com) and YOME (yogameditationhome.com), or check out YouTube channels like Yoga With Adriene and Fightmaster Yoga.

4. *Start a regular mindfulness practice with your family or friends.* The support of fellow practitioners can be extremely useful in cultivating mindfulness in your life. Try some of the mindfulness practices in this book with your children or partner and see if it helps you stay on track with your own mindfulness practice.

5. *Follow a media diet that promotes mindfulness.* Today's media is packed with stressful subject matter, so it's important to establish boundaries so you can stay informed without getting overloaded. Set time limits on your media consumption and choose mindfulness-oriented media from organizations like Mindful (mindful.org), Sounds True (soundstrue.com), and Dharma Seed (dharmaseed.org) to keep you inspired.

6. *Find a few mindfulness experts that you like and follow their work.* Whether the teacher who wrote your favorite chapter in this book or a bestselling author like Jon Kabat-Zinn, mindfulness experts work hard to share their wisdom. Many have websites and travel often to give talks and teach at meditation centers. Others have written books or made their talks available online. Some, like Tara Brach, record regular podcasts, too.

7. *Try practicing short, guided meditations.* Even as a seasoned meditator, I have days when I need to lean on a guided meditation session for support. The Insight Timer app, Dharma Seed, and Mindful offer thousands of free, guided meditations. Try a few different meditations to get a sense of which teachers and teaching styles might be a good fit for you.

8. *Sign up for a beginner's meditation class near you.* A quick Google search for "meditation class" or "mindfulness class" in your city may turn up some promising results at local meditation centers. Alternatively, you can look for an online meditation class or check with your local hospital or health-care network to see if they offer MBSR classes.

9. *Give yourself the gift of a mindfulness retreat.* Sometimes learning mindfulness is easiest in a retreat setting—one that lasts more than a day. Going on a meditation or yoga retreat allows you to practice mindfulness in an environment with fewer distractions, and it provides you with the opportunity to connect with a teacher and ask questions about your practice. Do a Google search for "beginner mindfulness retreat" to find retreats in your area.

10. *Join a local meditation group.* In Buddhism, practicing mindfulness in a community with other dedicated practitioners is viewed as an integral part of one's individual practice. Unlike meditation classes, which are for formal meditation instruction, meditation groups are places where people gather to sit in silent meditation together. You can find meditation groups near you on the Insight Timer app or by searching "meditation" on Meetup (meetup.com).

Resources

Chapter One: The Mindful Moment

Books & Publications

Bush, Mirabai Ed. *Contemplation Nation: How Ancient Practices Are Changing the Way We Live. Papers from The State of Contemplative Practice in America.* Kalamazoo: Fetzer Institute, 2011.

Chödrön, Pema. *When Things Fall Apart: Heart Advice for Difficult Times.* Boston: Shambhala Publications, 2011.

Ferguson, Gaylon. *Natural Wakefulness: Discovering the Wisdom We Were Born With.* Boston: Shambhala Publications, 2011.

Nhat Hanh, Thich. *Creating True Peace: Ending Violence in Yourself, Your Family, Your Community, and the World.* New York: Free Press, 2003.

Nhat Hanh, Thich. *You Are Here: Discovering the Magic of the Present Moment.* Boston: Shambhala Publications, 2010.

Salzberg, Sharon. *Lovingkindness: The Revolutionary Art of Happiness.* Boston: Shambala Publications, 2011.

Organizations & Websites

East Bay Meditation Center: East Bay Meditation Center's mission is to foster liberation, personal and interpersonal healing, social action, and inclusive community building. They offer mindfulness practices and teachings on wisdom and compassion from Buddhist and other spiritual traditions. EastBayMeditation.org.

Insight Timer: Home to more than 1,000,000 meditators, Insight Timer is rated as the top free meditation app on the Android and iOS stores. InsightTimer.com.

Lion's Roar: Lion's Roar brings you timeless Buddhist teachings, up-to-the-moment news, advice, and commentary, and Buddhist wisdom for our times. LionsRoar.com.

Mindful: Mindful's purpose is to inform, inspire, guide, and connect all those who want to live a mindful life, to enjoy the scientifically supported benefits of mindfulness practices, and to create a more mindful and caring society. Mindful.org.

Naropa University: This private liberal arts university in Colorado integrates Eastern wisdom studies with traditional Western scholarship. Naropa.edu. Brenda Salgado, the editor for *Real World Mindfulness for Beginners*, delivered the commencement address to Naropa graduates in May of 2016. A link to her speech is here: youtu.be/unmNWiqVOIY?t=1768.

Spirit Rock Meditation Center: Spirit Rock Meditation Center provides silent meditation retreats, classes, trainings, and Dharma study opportunities for new and experienced students from diverse backgrounds. SpiritRock.org.

Chapter Two: Regaining Focus and Concentration

Books & Publications

Gorman, Paul, and Ram Dass. *How Can I Help? Stories and Reflections on Service.* New York: Alfred A. Knopf, 2005.

Suzuki, Shunryū. *Zen Mind, Beginner's Mind*, 40th Anniversary Ed. Boston: Shambhala, 2010.

Tolle, Eckhart. *The Power of Now*. Novato, CA: New World Library, 1999.

Organizations & Websites

Eco-Cycle: Eco-Cycle offers a good compilation of how to reduce unwanted solicitations in our mailboxes: ecocycle.org.

Chapter Three: Cultivating Gratitude and Joy

Books & Publications

Achor, Shawn. *The Happiness Advantage: The Seven Principles of Positive Psychology That Fuel Success and Performance at Work*. New York: Crown Publishing Group, 2010.

Macy, Joanna, and Chris Johnstone. *Active Hope*. Novato, CA: New World Library, 2012.

Nhat Hanh, Thich. *Happiness: Essential Mindfulness Practices*. Berkeley, CA: Parallax Press, 2005.

Zinser, Annabelle. "Beginning Anew: A Mindfulness Practice for Communicating Appreciation." http://www.themindfulword.org/2013/beginning-anew -mindfulness-communicating-appreciation/. Accessed August 23, 2016.

Organizations & Websites

Plum Village Mindfulness Practice Center: This internationally-known meditation center was founded by Thich Nhat Hanh. Plumvillage.org.

Mindfulness Bell *Magazine:* The *Mindfulness Bell* is a journal of the art of mindful living, published three times a year. It also has an international list of all local meditation groups in the Thich Nhat Hanh tradition. Mindfulnessbell.org.

Wake Up: This active and global community brings together young mindfulness practitioners who want to create a healthy and compassionate society. Wkup.org

Wake Up Schools: This initiative hopes to cultivate mindfulness in education. It is a global vision to walk the path of compassion, peace, and joy in education through the practice of mindfulness. Wakeupschools.org

"Cultivating Happiness," *Network of Wellbeing.* www.youtube.com /watch?v=rTM5X4iQoMM.

"Five Ways to Become Happier Today," video by Tal Ben-Shahar. *YouTube.* www.youtube.com/watch?v=fLhpyzVTc8A.

"How to Cultivate Joy and Happiness," a video by Kaira Jewel Lingo. (in her earlier form as Sr. Jewel). *YouTube.* www.youtube.com/watch?v=AYoclMs7rqU.

"The Happiness Advantage: Linking Positive Brains to Performance," TEDxBloomington with Shawn Achor. *TEDxTalks.* www.youtube.com /watch?v=GXy__kBVq1M.

Chapter Six: Breaking Bad Habits or Negative Behaviors

Books & Publications

Cameron, Julia. *The Artist's Way.* New York: Jeremy P. Tarcher/Penguin, 2002. (For more on "Morning Pages," visit http://juliacameronlive.com/basic-tools /morning-pages/)

Kornfield, Jack. *The Art of Forgiveness, Lovingkindness, and Peace.* New York: Bantam, 2008.

Organizations & Websites

Dharma Punx Nation: Also called Against the Stream Buddhist Meditation Society, this organization offers classes, programs, and retreats, as well as private mindfulness instructions. Founded by Noah Levine, the author of *Refuge Recovery: A Buddhist Path to Recovering from Addiction,* the organization also offers programs for those who may choose mindfulness as a path out of or managing their addictions: Dharmapunx.com.

Insight Meditation Centers Worldwide: There is no requirement to be or become a Buddhist to attend any of the listed meditation centers. These locations offer mindfulness and other types of meditation practices. Buddhanet.net /medlinks.htm.

"The Habit Change Cheatsheet: 29 Ways to Successfully Ingrain a Behavior" by Leo Babauta—http://zenhabits.net/the-habit-change-cheatsheet-29 -ways-to-successfully-ingrain-a-behavior/

"These 3 Pages Might Be Your Key to a Clearer Mind, Better Ideas and Less Anxiety" by Chris Winfield—Take Back Your Life Blog: www.chriswinfield.com/morning-pages/

"Types of Meditation—An Overview of 23 Meditation Techniques" by Giovanni Dienstmann— Live and Dare Blog: http://liveanddare.com/types-of-meditation/

Chapter Seven: Working with Attachments and Aversions

Books & Publications

Ferguson, Gaylon. *Natural Wakefulness: Discovering the Wisdom We Were Born With.* Berkeley, CA: Shambhala, 2010.

Glassman, Bernie. *Bearing Witness: Stories of Martyrdom and Costly Discipleship.* Walden, NY: Plough Publishing House, 2016.

Maull, Fleet. *Dharma in Hell: The Prison Writings of Fleet Maull.* Providence, RI: Prison Dharma Network, 2005.

Mipham, Sakyong. *Ruling Your World: Ancient Strategies for Modern Life.* New York: Harmony, 2006.

Mipham, Sakyong. *Turning the Mind Into an Ally.* New York: Riverhead Books; reprint edition, 2004.

Trungpa, Chogyam. *Shambhala: The Sacred Path of the Warrior.* Berkeley, CA: Shambhala; reissued edition, 2007.

Organizations & Websites

Center for Mindfulness in Corrections: The Center for Mindfulness in Corrections offers a variety of mindfulness-based consulting and coaching services to correction agencies and agencies dealing with at-risk populations. Mindfulcorrections.org.

Engaged Mindfulness Institute: The Engaged Mindfulness Institute specializes in mindfulness-based emotional intelligence trainings for professionals and volunteers who support underserved populations and at-risk individuals and communities. Engagedmindfulness.org.

Mindful Justice Initiative: This initiative aims to create a criminal justice system grounded in mindfulness, compassion, and human dignity. Mindfuljustice.org.

Naropa University: This private liberal arts university in Colorado integrates Eastern wisdom studies with traditional Western scholarship. Naropa.edu.

Prison Mindfulness Institute: This nonprofit organization supports prisoners, prison staff, and prison volunteers with mindfulness-based tools for rehabilitation, self-transformation, and personal and professional development. Prisonmindfulness.org.

Shambhala: A Global Community: This international network of meditation centers brings together people who want to learn about mindfulness and contemplative arts. Shambhala.org.

Upaya Zen Center: The Center offers trainings, retreats, and programs for social and individual transformation, including the G.R.A.C.E.® training. Upaya.org.

Zen Peacemakers International: This is a nonprofit organization of socially engaged Buddhists. Zenpeacemakers.org.

Chapter Eight: Managing Anger and Hurt

Books & Publications

Chodron, Thubten. *Working with Anger*. Ithaca: Snow Lion Publications, 2001.

Hanh, Thich Nhat. *Anger: Wisdom for Cooling the Flames*. New York: Riverhead Books, 2001.

Makransky, John. *Awakening Through Love: Unveiling Your Deepest Goodness*. Somerville, MA: Wisdom Publications, 2007.

Williams, Angel Kyodo, Lama Rod Owens, and Jasmine Syedullah. *Radical Dharma: Talking Race, Love, and Liberation*. Berkeley: North Atlantic Books, 2016.

Chapter Nine: Supporting Others Who Need Help

Books & Publications

Kriseman, Nancy. *The Mindful Caregiver: Finding Ease in the Caregiving Journey.* Lanham, MD: Rowman & Littlefield, 2014.

Neff, Kristin. *Self-Compassion: The Proven Power of Being Kind to Yourself.* New York: HarperCollins, 2011.

Salzberg, Sharon. *The Kindness Handbook: A Practical Companion.* Boulder, CO: Sounds True, Inc., 2015.

Organizations & Websites

The Metta Institute: This organization provides educational programs and professional trainings that foster mindful and compassionate end-of-life care. Mettainstitute.org.

The Presence Care Project: They offer mindfulness-based dementia care training for family and professional caregivers. Presencecareproject.com/.

Self Compassion: Dr. Kristin Neff's website offers many resources on self-compassion, including articles and a directory of worldwide events and trainings. Selfcompassion.org.

Upaya Zen Center: The Center offers trainings, retreats, and programs for social and individual transformation, including the G.R.A.C.E.® training. Upaya.org.

Chapter Ten: Accepting Aging and Illness

Books & Publications

Boucher, Sandy. *Hidden Spring: A Buddhist Woman Confronts Cancer.* Somerville, MA: Wisdom Publications, 2000.

Lorde, Audre. *The Cancer Journals: Special Edition.* San Francisco: Aunt Lute Books, 1997.

Siff, Jason. *Unlearning Meditation: What to Do When the Instructions Get in the Way.* Boston: Shambhala Publications, 2010.

Tejaniya, Ashin. *Dhamma Everywhere: Welcoming Each Moment with Awareness + Wisdom.* Berkeley, CA: Wisdom Streams Foundation, 2014. (Also available for free at ashintejaniya.org.)

References

Chapter Two

Tolle, Eckhart. *A New Earth*. New York: Dutton/Penguin Group, 2005.

Chapter Three

APS. "Grin and Bear It! Smiling Facilitates Stress Recovery." www.psychologicalscience.org/index.php/news/releases/smiling-facilitates-stress-recovery.html. Accessed August 8, 2016.

Basaraba, Sharon. "How to De-Stress with a Smile." www.verywell.com/beat-stress-with-a-smile-2223757. Accessed August 8, 2016.

Fredrickson, Barbara L. "The Role of Positive Emotions in Positive Psychology." www.ncbi.nlm.nih.gov/pmc/articles/PMC3122271. Accessed August 8, 2016.

Hanson, Rick, PhD. "Overcoming the Negativity Bias." www.rickhanson.net/overcoming-negativity-bias. Accessed August 8, 2016.

Malcolm, Lynne. "Scientific evidence points to importance of positive thinking." www.abc.net.au. http://www.abc.net.au/radionational/programs/allinthemind/the-scientific-evidence-for-positive-thinking/6553614. Accessed August 8, 2016.

Nhat Hanh, Thich. *Present Moment, Wonderful Moment: Mindfulness Verses for Daily Living*. Berkeley, CA: Parallax Press, 2007.

Stibich, Mark, PhD. "Top 10 Reasons You Should Smile Every Day: Why Smiling Is So Powerful." www.verywell.com/top-reasons-to-smile-every-day-2223755. Accessed August 5, 2016.

Chapter Four

Carson, J. W. et al. "Loving-Kindness Meditation for Chronic Low Back Pain: Results from a Pilot Trial." www.ncbi.nlm.nih.gov/pubmed/16049118. Accessed August 10, 2016.

Fredrickson, Barbara L. et al. "The Role of Positive Emotions in Positive Psychology." www.ncbi.nlm.nih.gov/pmc/articles/PMC3122271/. Accessed August 8, 2016.

Kearney, David J. et al. "Loving-Kindness Meditation for Posttraumatic Stress Disorder: A Pilot Study." http://www.ncbi.nlm.nih.gov/pubmed/23893519. Accessed August 10, 2016.

Tonelli, Makenzie E. et al. "Meditation-Based Treatment Yielding Immediate Relief for Meditation-Naïve Migraineurs." http://www.ncbi.nlm.nih.gov /pubmed/24602422/. Accessed August 10, 2016.

Chapter Five

Ferguson, Gaylon. *Natural Bravery: Fear and Fearlessness as a Direct Path to Awakening*. Berkeley, CA: Shambhala Publications, 2016.

Ferguson, Gaylon. *Natural Wakefulness: Discovering the Wisdom We Were Born With*. Berkeley, CA: Shambhala Publications, 2009.

Sakyong Mipham. *Ruling Your World: Ancient Strategies for Modern Life*. New York: Morgan Road, 2005.

Sakyong Mipham. *Turning the Mind into an Ally*. New York: Riverhead Books, 2003.

Trungpa, Chögyam. *Shambhala: The Sacred Path of the Warrior*. Berkeley, CA: Shambhala Publications, 1978.

Trungpa, Chögyam. *The Heart of the Buddha*. Berkeley, CA: Shambhala Publications, 2010.

Shambhala: A Global Community—shambhala.org.

Chapter Six

Harper, J. "Day Five Metta: Forgiveness." dharmaseed.org/talks/audio _player/549/33610.html. Accessed July 25, 2016.

Ikeda-Nash, M. *Birthing and Blooming: Reflections on the Third Noble Truth*. In E. b. Gutierrez, "Dharma, Color, and Culture." Berkeley: Parallax Press, 2004.

Psychology Today. "Mindfulness: Present Moment Awareness." https://www. psychologytoday.com/basics/mindfulness. Accessed July 25, 2016.

Yang, Larry. "Be Inspired: Live Your Life with Awareness." http://www. huffingtonpost.com/larry-yang/be-inspiredlive-your-life_b_1411566.html. Accessed July 25, 2016.

Chapter Eight

Hanson, Rick, PhD. "Overcoming the Negativity Bias." www.rickhanson.net /overcoming-negativity-bias. Accessed August 8, 2016.

Chapter Nine

Goleman, Daniel. "Wired for Kindness: Science shows we prefer compassion, and our capacity grows with practice." *Washington Post*. https://www .washingtonpost.com/news/inspired-life/wp/2015/06/23/wired-for -kindness-science-shows-we-prefer-compassion-and-our-capacity -grows-with-practice. Accessed July 20, 2016.

Solon, Olivia. "Compassion over empathy could help prevent burnout." *Wired* (blog). www.wired.co.uk/article/tania-singer-compassion-burnout. Accessed July 20, 2016.

Index of Mindfulness Practices

Index

Hanson, Rick, 96
happiness
    cultivating, 38–42
    expanding capacity for, 40
Hayashi, Arawana, 142
health, appreciating, 129
health challenges, and mindfulness, 14
heart, making space in, 138–139
helping others
    and mindfulness, 112–113
    random acts of kindness, 48–49
    self-care and self-compassion, 113–114
hurt beneath anger, contacting, 106–107

I

illness and aging
    Gratitude for Life practice, 128–129
    and mindfulness, 124
    responding to, 125
    Taking a Pause practice, 130–131
impatience, recognizing, 52
instant gratification, 38
intentions
    caring with, 118–119
    setting, 78, 80–81

J

Jikoji Zen Center, 164
Johnson, Kate, 133, 169
journaling daily, 84–85
joy, increasing, 48–49
judgment, noticing, 52

K

Kabat-Zinn, Jon, 15, 19, 147
kindness, showing, 25, 48–49. *See also* loving-kindness; self-kindness
Kornfield, Jack, 55, 115

L

Lingo, Kaira Jewel, 37, 165
Lion's Roar Foundation, 13
Liu, Yingzhao, 27, 164

loss, Mindful Movement
    practice, 142–143
loss and grief
    establishing personal ritual, 140–141
    Making Space in the Heart
        practice, 138–139
    and mindfulness, 134–135
    pain of, 133
    responding to, 135–136
love, experiencing feelings of, 24
loving-kindness. *See also* kindness; self-kindness
    meditation, 61
    sending wishes of, 117

M

Maull, Fleet, 87, 167
MBSR (Mindfulness-Based Stress
    Reduction), 15, 124
media diet, following, 147
meditation. *See also* breath meditation
    joining group, 147
    versus mindfulness, 15
    practicing, 147–148
    trying, 29
mindfulness
    and anger, 100–101
    and attachments, 88–89
    and being judgmental, 52
    committing to daily practice, 146
    concept of, 14
    defined, 10
    of fear, 64, 71
    finding experts on, 147
    going on retreat, 147
    and gratitude, 39–40
    and health challenges, 14
    and helping others, 112–113
    and impatience, 52
    and loss, 134–135
    versus meditation, 15
    myths about, 15–16

About the Contributors

Brenda Salgado is founder and Director of the Nepantla Center for Healing and Renewal and has over 20 years of experience in non-profit management. She is active in bringing mindfulness and spiritual practices to leaders, diverse communities, and social justice organizations. Trained by elders in traditional medicine, Brenda draws on the healing powers of the natural world to guide her work as a spiritual leader and healer. She serves on the boards of Movement Strategy Center and the Lion's Roar Foundation. In the past, she has worked for East Bay Meditation Center, Movement Strategy Center, and Breast Cancer Action. Her current projects are focused on sacred economics, transformational leadership, and indigenous teachings for our times. She is committed to co-creating a society filled with wholeness and beauty, and is grateful to her ancestors for the values that have led her to spiritual, healing, and social justice work. To learn more, visit nepantlaconsulting.com

Yingzhao Liu is a design director for international markets at LinkedIn in Mountain View, CA, and in her free time serves as an experiential educator and facilitator on topics of communication and transformation. She is also a resident and board member of Jikoji Zen Center. Yingzhao is native to mainland China and has traveled to five continents and thirty countries. She is often affirmed by people's relationships to the environment they live in—their creativity and spirituality in everyday life. To learn more, visit linkedin.com/in/yingzhao.

Kaira Jewel Lingo is a mindfulness teacher based in Washington, D.C. She leads retreats in the United States and internationally, offering mindfulness programs for educators and youth in schools as well as people of color, artists, activists, and ecologists. She aspires to create an urban mindfulness center in the District of Columbia for diverse and underserved people. An ordained nun of 15 years in Thich Nhat Hanh's Order of Interbeing, she edited Thich Nhat Hanh's, *Planting Seeds: Practicing Mindfulness with Children* and helped start and develop Wake Up Schools, an initiative to cultivate mindfulness in education. She explores the interweaving of art, play, activism, and spiritual practice and is a certified yoga teacher and InterPlay leader. In spring 2015 and 2016, she was spiritual practitioner in residence at Schumacher College, an ecological college in the United Kingdom. To learn more, visit kairajewel.com.

Jacoby Ballard is an educator, teacher, activist, and writer known for his playfulness, heart-opening, and commitment to change from the inside out. He has been practicing yoga and Buddhism for 20 years as tools for survival and resilience. As an antiracist, white genderqueer person, he has a specific interest in applying the teachings of yoga for social justice and the liberation of all beings. He cofounded Third Root Community Health Center and serves on the Advisory Board of the Yoga Service Council. Jacoby is known for teaching and developing programs on Diversity Training for Yoga Teachers, LGBT, Queer and Trans Yoga, Yoga for Survivors and Yoga for Recovery, as well as working with yoga and plants to heal the trauma of oppression. To learn more, visit jacobyballard.com.

Acharya Gaylon Ferguson, PhD is a senior teacher (acharya) in the Shambhala Buddhist tradition. He led his first month-long group meditation retreat in 1976 according to the instructions he practices under his teachers, Tibetan Buddhist meditation masters Chögyam Trungpa Rinpoche and Sakyong Mipham Rinpoche. A Fulbright Fellow to Nigeria, he received his doctorate in anthropology from Stanford University. After teaching cultural anthropology at the University of Washington, he joined the core faculty of Naropa University in 2006. He is the author of *Natural Wakefulness* and *Natural Bravery* as well as numerous articles in *Buddhadharma, Tricycle, Shambhala Sun*, and *Lion's Roar*. His writings have twice been selected for inclusion in *The Best Buddhist Writing* annual series. He authored "Buddhism and the Politics of Race," a chapter in the collection *Mindful Politics*, published by Simon & Schuster in 2012.

Fresh! White is a professional certified coach, facilitator, and mindfulness teacher. As a coach, he supports executives, entrepreneurs, artists, and other coaches with achieving their goals. Through mindfulness and value alignment, Fresh! helps clients see clearly through their fears and improve their emotional responses to challenging situations, which supports and strengthens their efficiency at school and work, and expands their creativity in all areas of their life. Fresh! is a contributor to *Trans Bodies, Trans Selves: A Resource for the Transgender Community,* and has facilitated more than 150 trans and LGBTQ ally workshops. He is a student in Spirit Rock's Community Dharma Leaders Program, founded a Trans & Genderqueer Mindfulness Meetup group in the San Francisco Bay Area, and is co-teacher for the East Bay Meditation Center's Family Sangha. To learn more, visit affirmativeacts.org.

Acharya Fleet Maull is an empowered senior Dharma teacher in the global Shambhala Meditation Community and the international Zen Peacemakers. He is an author, prison activist, trainer, and executive coach. He founded the Prison Mindfulness Institute and the National Prison Hospice Association and cofounded the Engaged Mindfulness Institute and the Upaya Institute Buddhist Chaplaincy Training Program. He is the author of *Dharma in Hell: The Prison Writings of Fleet Maull* and the forthcoming *Radical Responsibility*. Acharya Maull began practicing mindfulness meditation in the early 1970s, seeking a deeper context for his life; he later embraced the practice even more deeply during his prison years to transform his addictions and support his fellow prisoners. Acharya Maull is a frequent presenter at conferences in the mindfulness and criminal justice fields and leads meditation retreats, transformational seminars, prison programs, and bearing witness retreats throughout the world. To learn more, visit fleetmaull.com.

Lama Rod Owens is an activist, organizer, poet, and authorized Dharma teacher in the Tibetan tradition of Buddhism. He is a core teacher with Natural Dharma Fellowship and is a master of divinity candidate at Harvard Divinity School where he studies the intersection of Buddhism, contemplative practice, identity, and social change. Known for his authentic teaching style of self inquiry and humor, he has appeared in several publications, including *Lion's Roar, Buddhadharma, Tricycle,* and *Harvard Divinity Bulletin*, and he has been recognized as one of the emerging leaders of the next generation of Dharma teachers. He is also a coauthor of *Radical Dharma: Taking Race, Love, and Liberation*, which explores race and oppression within American Buddhist communities. To learn more, visit lamarod.com.

Maia Duerr is a writer, anthropologist, and ordained chaplain who teaches reflective practices that cultivate compassion, awareness, and social transformation. Maia collaborated with Dr. Joan Halifax to envision the Upaya Zen Center Buddhist Chaplaincy Training Program and directed the program from 2008 to 2014. Prior to that, she was the research director at the Center for Contemplative Mind in Society where she worked with mindfulness teacher Mirabai Bush to document the use of contemplative practices in secular settings. Maia is the author of numerous articles and essays. Her forthcoming book, *Fall in Love with Your Work: A Mindfulness-Based Guide to Creating Right Livelihood,* will be published by Parallax Press in 2017. To learn more about Maia's work, visit maiaduerr.com.

Shahara Godfrey, PhD is an African-American/Bajan woman, a mother, and a grandmother. She is also a recent cancer survivor. She has practiced in the Theravada Buddhist tradition for over 20 years, with primary practices in compassion and social activism. She received her PhD in Humanities with a focus on Transformative Learning and Change from the California Institute of Integral Studies, and is a graduate of the UCLA Mindful Awareness Research Center program. She is a core teacher at the East Bay Meditation Center and has completed the Community Dharma Leaders and Dedicated Practitioners programs at the Spirit Rock Insight Meditation Center. She enjoys coaching students who are working on their dissertations and teaching mindfulness to those coping with aging and illness. To learn more, visit mindfuldissertation.com.

Kate Johnson has taught mindful yoga and meditation in schools, health centers, and with social change agents and communities for over a decade. Currently, she co-teaches the meditation teacher training and offers engaged Buddhist studies programs at the Interdependence Project. She also trains yoga teachers who work in public schools with the organization Bent on Learning. A lifelong dancer, Kate holds a BFA in dance from The Ailey School/Fordham University and an MA in Performance Studies from New York University. Kate's forthcoming book about waking up to power and oppression as a spiritual practice will be published by Parallax Press in 2017.